WITHDRAWN

Superpowers for Parents

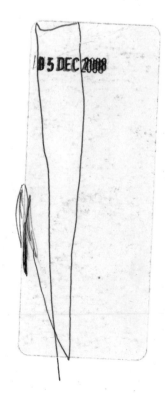

Prentice Hall LIFE

If life is what you make it, then making it better starts here.

What we learn today can change our lives tomorrow. It can change our goals or change our minds; open up new opportunities or simply inspire us to make a difference. That's why we have created a new breed of books that do more to help you make more of *your* life.

Whether you want more confidence or less stress, a new skill or a different perspective, we've designed *Prentice Hall Life* books to help you to make a change for the better. Together with our authors we share a commitment to bring you the brightest ideas and best ways to manage your life, work and wealth.

In these pages we hope you'll find the ideas you need for the life *you* want. Go on, help yourself.

It's what you make it

* * *

Superpowers
for Parents

The psychology of great parenting and happy children

Dr Stephen Briers

Harlow, England • London • New York • Boston • San Francisco • Toronto • Sydney • Singapore • Hong Kong
Tokyo • Seoul • Yapei • New Delhi • Cape Town • Madrid • Mexico City • Amsterdam • Munich • Paris • Milan

Pearson Education Limited

Edinburgh Gate
Harlow CM20 2JE
Tel: +44 (0)1279 623623
Fax: +44 (0)1279 431059
Website: www.pearsoned.co.uk

First published in Great Britain in 2008

© Dr Stephen Briers 2008

The right of Dr Stephen Briers to be identified as author of this work has been asserted by him in accordance with the Copyright, Designs and Patents Act 1988.

ISBN: 978-0-273-71435-4

British Library Cataloguing-in-Publication Data
A catalogue record for this book is available from the British Library

Library of Congress Cataloging-in-Publication Data
A catalog record for this book is available from the Library of Congress

Photograph on page 62 by Rebecca Ellis/www.istockphoto.com

10 9 8 7 6 5 4 3 2 1
12 11 10 09 08

Text design by Design Deluxe, Bath
Typeset in 11pt Classical Garamond by 3
Printed and bound in Great Britain by Ashford Colour Press Ltd, Gosport, Hants

The publisher's policy is to use paper manufactured from sustainable forests.

For my family

Acknowledgements

G rateful thanks to my colleagues John McKeown and Dr Kate Alexander for their support and insightful comments during the writing of this book. I would also like to thank Emma Shackleton for getting it commissioned and my brilliant editor, Rachael Stock, who has managed to juggle the demands of small children and recalcitrant authors with equal aplomb. Special thanks to my very dear wife, Mel, who always underestimates her own superpowers, but has come to my rescue more times than I can count. Finally, I want to thank my boys, Joe and Will, for making me proud to be their father and helping me want to become a better one. And yes, Joe, I really *am* a psychologist ...

Author's note

A few words about the way the book is written. Although you will find some examples involving children I have met in my clinical work, naturally I have changed names and certain details to protect their anonymity. Occasionally I have featured cases that are a compilation of several real children because this turned out to be the best way to draw out the relevant points.

Grammatically, I have used the pronouns 'he' and 'she' interchangeably throughout the text. This isn't just about political correctness: it's very hard to do anything else. Please mentally translate this into the language that relates to the gender of your own children.

Chapters 2 to 7 each contain one central topic and a cluster of related skills. However, as you will see, there are many themes that run throughout the book and a number of the techniques described can be applied in a range of different contexts. Please feel free to think flexibly about how you can make the content most relevant to your child's life.

Most of the specific techniques described in the book are taken from standard clinical practice. These are the sorts of things you and your child would be taught should you ever visit a child clinical psychologist in a professional capacity. I can take personal credit for very few of the ideas in this book, but what I hope I have done is present the current research and state-of-the-art clinical strategies in a clear and accessible form that will allow you as a parent to begin applying these techniques as part of your childrearing.

If you do find yourself struggling can I encourage you not to give up but consult someone who may be able to help you become proficient with these tools? There are also lots of helpful guides out there and I have included suggestions for further reading should you feel you need more support or information.

Finally, I hope reading this book is an enjoyable experience for you. The minds of children offer a fascinating world to explore, and I hope you will find things in the following pages that will inspire as well as inform.

Contents

Introduction

Parenting is not easy. However much we love our children, and however much joy they bring, sometimes they push us to our limits. We are left feeling emotionally, mentally and physically drained. At such moments what parent *wouldn't* wish for superpowers? How fantastic it would be if we could instantly transform our children's behaviour, make them see sense or magically erase their troubles.

Unfortunately even this book can't make it quite that easy. There are no magic wands, no quick-fix solutions, no one-size-fits-all answers. However, before you rush off to the bookseller to demand your refund, consider this: perhaps we parents are not the ones most in need of such superpowers? What difference would it make to our children's lives (and ours) if *they* were more capable of managing themselves in the very situations that end up running us ragged?

This book is designed to help parents equip children to cope better with life. You may not be able to bestow super-human powers on your offspring but you certainly can teach skills, tactics and strategies that will significantly increase your child's own capacity for self-control. I know from experience that if children learn to apply such tools consistently the results can be dramatic.

Training children to develop these 'superpowers' is most effective when done daily, and they can be introduced when children are still very young. It's important to stress that this is a proactive way of parenting, not a reactive one.

Instead of waiting for bad behaviour to surface and then having to deal with it, there are skills we can teach our children that will help reduce the likelihood of that bad behaviour happening in the first place. And – rather magically – these same skills and abilities will also help children feel happier, less pressurized by life and more able to deal with their own feelings, other people and the world around them.

None of the superpowers have to be taught in a formal sense. In fact they are best introduced gently, without drawing attention to them, as part of daily life. The aim of this book is to provide you with the ideas and the know-how so that when tricky situations do crop up, or when you sense a storm brewing, you are already prepared and primed with all the strategies and skills you need to deal deftly with the situation.

The rise of the guilty parent

Previous generations of parents would probably shake their heads in wonder at the idea of us all striving to be better parents. In the old days, childrearing was just common sense or a traditional way of doing things, handed down largely unquestioned from one generation to the next. It used to be that parents were simply parents. It was their children who were more likely to be labelled 'good' or 'bad'. All that has changed. Since the 1960s it has become almost heretical to suggest that a child might be held personally responsible for her more undesirable behaviour.

The explanation for this shift lies with the 'Behaviourists'. Building on the work of Pavlov (of drooling dog fame) and John B. Watson, from the 1930s onwards psychologists like B. F. Skinner championed the extreme position that all human behaviour could be reduced to a fixed chain of cause and effect. Behind the smokescreen of the liberal, free-thinking 1960s, these 'behaviourist' assumptions were infiltrating every aspect of our thinking – and nowhere more strongly than in our beliefs about parenting.

The end result is that we now see the badly behaved child as the victim of an inadequate or flawed upbringing. If *only* the parents had been more consistent ... If *only* they had set and maintained boundaries ... Handled differently, it surely stands to reason that little Laura would now be a model citizen and not the obnoxious delinquent she has become? While there may be some truth in this, there is a real danger that such a simplistic view does little justice to either Laura or her parents. This kind of approach encourages us to think of children as biological machines to be programmed, rather than sentient human beings struggling to make sense of themselves and their environment.

However, the outcome is that our parenting, like so many aspects of modern life, is now subject to constant scrutiny and evaluation from both within and without. Never has parenting been such a self-conscious and guilt-stricken affair. We strive to do the best we can, and when our children do misbehave we feel we have little choice but to point the finger squarely back at ourselves.

Developments from ASBOs to TV programmes play to such anxieties and often reinforce a behavioural analysis of the problem. Bad parenting is always to blame. The media (and as a contributor to various BBC parenting series I must put my hands up here) offer endless advice on 'fixing' problem behaviour using practical behavioural techniques ranging from star charts to naughty steps. The continuing popularity of such TV programmes testifies to the sincere desire of parents to do their best for their children, the universality of the struggle with defiant and difficult behaviour, and the underlying insecurity that sometimes leads us to compare ourselves with other mums and dads. We all want to get it right.

Although the techniques shown on such programmes are genuinely helpful, they do sometimes create the misleading impression that star charts and naughty steps are the solution to all our children's problems.

Moving beyond the 'carrot and stick' approach

I want to make it clear that I am by no means opposed to behaviourist approaches *per se*. The use of such techniques has been tremendously empowering for many parents and provided them with effective strategies for calming troubled domestic waters. Children undoubtedly *do* respond well to suitable boundaries, and the judicious administration of carrot and stick does have an important role in good parenting. In my clinics I regularly recommend such approaches as an important aspect of supporting a child's development and emotional adjustment.

But this is precisely my point: however important they are, conditioning techniques represent only *one* aspect of the bigger picture. Our society is in increasing danger of mistaking the part for the whole and developing a fixation on the symptom rather than the cause. Is the highest accolade of our parenting really the eradication of 'problem behaviour'? Are we losing sight of the important truth behind Jess Lair's astute (if slightly twee) observation that: 'Children are not things to be moulded, but are people to be unfolded'?

A shift in the parenting agenda is long overdue. We need to move the focus away from the containment of problem behaviour after it surfaces and pay more attention to developing the psychological skills children need to manage their lives. Prevention really *is* better than cure and, if we can equip children with the relevant skills, they stand a good chance of heading off not only their own bad behaviour but a host of potential mental health problems before they take root.

Protecting your child's mind

There is certainly good cause to suggest that as parents we do need to be thinking about how we can protect the mental health of the next generation. Surveys and statistics are released on an almost weekly basis indicating that mental illness of all kinds is on the increase and that young people may be especially vulnerable. The evidence suggests that there are more depressed children in our midst than ever before and that the average onset of the emotional disorders is happening earlier.

A UK Department of Health survey in 2004 established that within a comprehensive sample of British children 8 per cent of 5–10 year olds were suffering from a diagnosable mental disorder, a total which had risen to nearly 12 per cent within the 11–15 age bracket.

On the other side of the Atlantic, Professor Martin Seligman's rigorous analysis of four large-scale American studies across different age groups leads him to similarly alarming conclusions; namely that since the 1950s there has been 'more depression, beginning younger and younger . . .' Seligman refers to an 'epidemic of depression' and points out how crucial it is that preventative steps are taken to counter its debilitating impact amongst young people.

In view of such figures it seems clear that modern parents *must* now be thinking beyond the control of bad behaviour, especially since (particularly in the case of boys) acting-up behaviour itself may be symptomatic of underlying emotional disturbance.

What Seligman and colleagues found is that by cultivating specific habits of thought using simple cognitive behavioural techniques it is possible to provide children with a level of psychological innoculation against depressive illness. These techniques are simple to teach and have been carefully assessed to establish their effectiveness. There is no reason why all children should not be taught these skills to help safeguard their mental health in the same way that as parents we teach them how to brush their teeth to stop them getting tooth decay.

Of course, the value of teaching psychological life skills to kids is not just about preventing things going wrong, but giving children tools that can enhance their sense of competence, self-esteem and fulfilment. Over the past few decades the Positive Psychology movement has produced some revealing insights into what makes people happy and emotionally well balanced. We now have a much better idea of what skills and mindsets promote happiness and well-being, and we know that these skills/mindsets can be learned. This book will show you how to help your children develop them.

What does 'discipline' really mean?

It is a widely held view that the children of the Playstation generation are less well disciplined than their predecessors. However, we tend to ignore the fact that the word 'discipline' has several meanings. It is now generally associated with correction and punishment, but the original Latin root of the word *disciplina* implies a mentoring relationship: the pupil or 'disciple' submits to instruction in order to hone his skills and realize his potential. This is an aspect of discipline we are at risk of neglecting in modern parenting.

Having worked clinically with children, my conviction is that if we can teach our children how to recognize and manage their own thoughts and feelings at a much earlier age, then the 'problem behaviour' that preoccupies our current concept of childrearing might actually become less of a problem for all of us. If we invest in equipping them with the mental tools they need, our children will become less reliant on bad behaviour and find more productive ways to resolve their problems.

Already I can hear you thinking to yourself: 'This sounds all very well in theory but has he forgotten that we are talking about *children* here ... ? Don't the skills referred to require a level of sophistication well beyond the scope of most youngsters?' The answer on both counts is fortunately 'no'.

In the first place, despite what professional clinicians might have you believe, much of the more practical end of psychology is hardly rocket science. Clinicians routinely teach many of these techniques to children in their consulting rooms. Sadly, however, the children concerned are not usually equipped with these skills until things have become bad enough for their parents or teachers to seek professional help.

With a little creativity, the skills concerned can also be taught in different ways at different levels of complexity according to the age and capacity of your child. One of the aims of this book will be to demonstrate how the techniques described can be adapted to make them relevant even to very young children. If their protective and life-enhancing benefits are to be maximized, ideally the foundation of these skills can and should be laid at a much earlier age than you might assume possible. While practical experience suggests that even young children can master these techniques, new research findings also suggest that children are far more competent and capable than we have previously been led to believe.

Your amazing child

Perhaps one of the most damaging legacies of Behaviourism has been the blinkered vision it has given us of children themselves. Although the discipline of psychology has happily moved on, the sad reality is that in parenting circles we continue to treat children like little 'black boxes'. Their internal workings are allowed to remain a mystery while we both discredit and underestimate their intelligence. We tend not to see children as young minds striving to make sense of their world, but as bundles of impulses, appetites and reflexes that in Lair's words must be 'moulded' towards social conformity.

Unfortunately it is not just Behaviourism that has biased our conception of childhood but, ironically, a branch of developmental psychology that seems at first glance to offer an antidote to the limitations of the behaviourist approach. Unlike many psychologists of his day, Jean Piaget was deeply interested in the child's mental world. His great contribution was a vision of a child's intelligence expanding progressively through a succession of stages, each representing an extension and refinement of the stage before.

The field of child development owes a great debt to Piaget – he made huge contributions to our understanding. Unfortunately, however, his stages of development are tied fairly rigidly to ages, and led us to make assumptions about what children are capable of understanding, and when. The trouble is that such expectations have a tendency to become self-fulfilling. If we assume a younger child cannot hope to grasp a concept we make no effort to teach it: because we do not teach it the child never demonstrates the skill and thus reinforces our belief that he is incapable of learning it.

The exciting twist in the story is that the latest experimental research is suggesting that even very young infants have far greater intellectual powers than was ever assumed possible. Meanwhile, new findings in the field of neuroscience bring us closer to understanding how this potential is to be unlocked.

For example, it now appears that infants as young as 3

to 4 months have the beginnings of a working knowledge of the physical world. They know that an object will fall if not supported and that a ball requires a push to set it in motion. Children as young as 5 months can actually count up to three.

More relevant for the purposes of this book, it also appears that young children have much greater capacity for abstract thinking than the theories of Piaget would allow. They are able to 'learn about learning', even from a very young age. There is experimental evidence that they can stand back and evaluate strategies used for solving problems, whereas previously it was assumed that they lacked the reflective abilities required to do this. Children don't simply rely on trial and error, repeatedly forcing the square peg into the round hole until it works. New findings suggest that in certain circumstances children are capable of much higher-level thinking than we formerly thought possible.

Many of the skills described in this book are geared towards helping children solve emotional and thinking problems. They require children to become aware of their own internal processes, and to figure out what works and what does not when they encounter difficulties in their mental and social worlds. Although clinical experience suggests that most children are more than up to the task when given appropriate support, it is reassuring that the research evidence confirms that these abilities lie comfortably within their grasp.

Too much like hard work?

Even if it is technically possible for children to master such skills, doesn't it drain some of the fun and spontaneity out of childhood? Isn't it all a bit serious? Shouldn't we let our children just enjoy being kids?

I would entirely agree that it is vital to give children the space and freedom to enjoy and discover themselves through unstructured play. We are right to distrust the kind of hot-housing of children that so often stems from insecurity or the invidious desire to compare children's accomplishments with those of neighbours or friends. Jokes about flashcards in the womb are sometimes a little close to home, and is there really any long-term advantage if my child learns to read a year ahead of her best friend?

However, to suggest that we shouldn't try and help improve our children's self-control and give them key psychological skills on the grounds that it takes the fun out of childhood suggests a misunderstanding of the kinds of skills we're talking about and perhaps a somewhat rose-tinted vision of what it's actually like to be a child.

Whether they are aware of it or not, parents teach their children all the time. Not only do children learn by observing us and following our example, but parents already help their children structure problems or help contain their anxieties and fears as a matter of course.

The techniques described in this book can all be used in this kind of daily, real-life situation. It shouldn't feel like hard work as they can be woven quite naturally into everyday living, at times when you'd normally be thinking about what to say to your child or how you could help them deal with what was happening. The tools and strategies will hopefully come alive for your children because they can be introduced within the context of practical, real-life situations as and when they are needed.

Is it not better to lay a careful foundation of 'right thinking' from the outset, rather than have to unpick destructive patterns at a later date? Good or bad, such habits will have many years to consolidate and anyone who has tried to break a habit of any kind already knows how difficult that can be. Is it not worth investing in a bit of informal mental coaching with your child to ensure that such bad habits never get a stranglehold in the first place?

We also need to bear in mind how easy it is for us to entertain romantic notions of what it is like to be a child. Contrary to popular belief, very few of us experience childhood as a carefree Elysium of endless summers and sweet, dreamless nights.

Just think about it for a moment: you are physically and intellectually punier than the adults all around you, and utterly dependent upon them for your bodily and emotional survival. You have precious little control over your life. All of the big decisions and many of the minor ones are made for you. As a rule you are expected to do what you are told regardless of what you might want. Frustratingly, you often do not even know what you *do* want. The world around you may be full of wonder but also reveals itself to be a place of unfathomable terrors. Unfortunately for you, you lack the experience to know which is which. The more you learn the more alarming it can all seem. To top it off your body keeps changing size and shape at an unpredictable rate and you find yourself at the mercy of powerful waves of emotion that can completely overwhelm you at a moment's notice.

Not sounding so appealing now? The whole point about improving your children's capacity for self-regulation is that you are helping empower one the world's most disenfranchised populations. Rather than stripping the magic out of childhood, the chances are that with these skills under their belt children will actually be in a better position to enjoy a more carefree and happy childhood, and hopefully a more carefree and happy adulthood to boot.

Teaching children psychological life skills from an early age is not only possible, but represents a sound investment in your child's happiness and mental well-being. Research now suggests children are equipped to learn, so now it's up to us as parents to equip ourselves to teach.

This book is designed to do just that – to introduce you to tools and concepts you should find useful in the quest to be a better parent. In applying them, hopefully we can all move a little further away from the naughty step.

It is time to expand our definition of 'good parenting'. We need a more proactive vision in which we take up the responsibility of equipping the next generation with the life skills they need to cope with the stresses of modern living. To do so effectively, our children need to be taught how to master both the challenges of the world around them and the equally demanding terrain of their own minds.

1
X-ray vision

What's going on inside?

P sychologists are trained to notice not only what their clients say and do, but also how their clients make them feel. This is called 'counter-transference' and can provide vital clues about the client's inner world. For example, if I find myself feeling inexplicably downcast before a certain client's sessions, this might tell me something about that client's own state of mind.

So what happens if we apply this principle of counter-transference to our encounters with misbehaving children? What do we typically feel as parents at such moments? And what can that tell us about how our children are feeling?

Speaking personally, the first thing I usually experience is a surge of internal pressure that, unless I am careful, prompts me to explode right back in their faces. The strength of feeling that even quite mild child misbehaviour can evoke is surprising. Whatever control I muster on the surface, I am conscious of an inner voice screaming that it has got to STOP before the internal pressure becomes unbearable. Quite irrationally, I can experience my kids' conduct as a violation of my boundaries, as an intrusion or an attack. I can even feel that things are starting to fall apart – literally disintegrating around me. At another level I also feel embarrassed, ashamed that their conduct has deviated so far from what it should be, from what *I* want it to be.

Every parent knows that the company of a screaming toddler can be a bizarrely humiliating experience. In my consulting rooms many parents confess that they have never felt as helpless as when unable to manage their children's behaviour. I suspect it is the unique power of our children to confront us at such times with our own buried vulnerabilities that can make parental discipline such an emotive issue for us all.

In the face of such uncomfortable feelings, the natural priority is to strike back and attempt to halt their disturbing behaviour as swiftly as possible. Dismissing a child as 'bad' under these circumstances is one tempting means of sealing off such distressing emotions and disconnecting ourselves from the source. However, while at such times we may want to distance ourselves emotionally from our children, it is important to consider our own reactions as a useful window onto what it is like for the child in the throes of the tantrum.

Scratch the surface of a badly behaved child's defiance and we probably find something not far removed from the adult's experience: a soul in some degree of torment, battling with a succession of gut-wrenching emotions; someone who feels helpless, ashamed and ultimately humiliated by his own lack of control.

There is a fantastic chapter in P. L. Travers' *Mary Poppins* called 'Bad Tuesday' in which Michael Banks wakes up with 'a curious feeling' inside him. Under the irresistible influence of this strange mood Michael diagnoses (quite correctly) that he is going to be naughty. And he certainly is. He is cheeky to Ellen the housemaid, Mrs Brill the cook, his mother and even – most thrillingly – to the formidable Mary Poppins herself.

Uncharacteristically, Mary Poppins largely ignores Michael's provocative behaviour. With the aid of a mysterious compass, she soon whisks the children to the four corners of the globe where they encounter respectively a polar bear, a hyacinth macaw, a panda and a dolphin. The children are given a warm and friendly welcome by the various animals. However, even the distraction of this magical mystery tour has little effect on Michael's glowering mood and deteriorating conduct. Eventually, he steals the compass and attempts to escape from his family. But unfortunately for Michael, Mary Poppins' grim prophecy that Master Banks has 'got something coming to him' proves alarmingly accurate. Michael unwittingly summons up a nightmarish vision of the four animals, this time incarnated as feral, vicious predators who bear down menacingly upon him from the four corners of the room. Michael drops the compass in terror and screams out for Mary Poppins. Predictably, she arrives on cue and order is smoothly restored.

Now a straightforward reading is that this is a tale of a wilful child who gets his just deserts. In what for the parental reader is a satisfying twist, Michael brings upon himself due retribution for his bad behaviour. However, what is so interesting about this chapter is the commentary it provides on the experience of such 'naughtiness' from the child's perspective.

What seems clear is that Michael is at the mercy of internal forces he cannot really control. Whilst he may put up little resistance, the strange feeling with which he awakes effectively drives him from one act of naughtiness to the next with an inevitable momentum. At various points he attempts to 'own' his deviance, resisting all attempts to make him feel apologetic and driving his bad behaviour forward, but the reality seems to be that in this state Michael has limited jurisdiction over his actions.

It is significant that the book's heroine, that reliable champion of decorum, good manners and a neatly turned-out appearance, makes so little attempt to rebuke him. Mary Poppins treats Michael as if he is in a state of diminished responsibility. Certainly, as matters deteriorate,

Michael seems to find himself cut adrift from familiar sources of support, both internal and external. He becomes unable to relate to the people or perspectives that might anchor him. Even Mary Poppins' reproach has little effect upon him. Eventually, Michael is reduced to a state of utter powerlessness and becomes easy prey for the terrifying phantasms he has unleashed.

The story is compelling for children, not least because they recognize the fundamental truth of Michael's plight: however deliberate it may look, to be caught up in the extremes of 'bad behaviour' involves a loss of self-control and is an experience that ushers in elements of genuine fear and disorientation. Michael may not put up a particularly good fight but P. L. Travers portrays him as much victim as perpetrator.

> Bad behaviour involves a loss of self-control and that can be a frightening and unpleasant experience for the child as well as the parent.

Closer to home

I remember an incident when, for some reason I cannot now even recall, my 10-year-old son erupted in anger and started swearing at me in front of his grandparents who were visiting at the time. I was shocked by the language, outraged about my son's rudeness, and mortified that this unsavoury episode was playing out in front of my wife's parents who (according to family lore) had magically conjured the highest standards of behaviour from their own three children. With a certain satisfaction I readied myself for the blast of frosty disapproval that my son was about to unleash from his grandparents.

Imagine then my surprise when instead his grandmother's eyes filled with tears and she started pleading with me to 'help him'. Now at this juncture the only 'help' I was picturing myself offering my son was being administered, Homer Simpson-style, with both hands firmly around his neck. However, what my mother-in-law recognized was something that the heat of my own indignation had hidden from me; namely that being as wound up as my son had become is actually a very threatening mental space to inhabit. As she explained to me later: 'I know what it's like to get into that place where you just can't get back again ...'

I am not implying that all children's bad behaviour should simply be excused or dismissed because of how upsetting it can be for them. On the contrary, a cornerstone of the approach in this book is that children should be encouraged to take *more* responsibility for their behaviour, not less. However, if we expect children to master their antisocial impulses we also need to give them the skills and techniques to do so.

All too often in the way we deal with children's tantrums or outbursts we talk to them as if they were simply electing to be defiant or difficult, and that it would be just as easy for them to 'switch off' their bad behaviour and simply choose to be 'good'. The reality is that even as adults we do not always find this easy, but for children impulse control is an especially demanding task.

If we want our children to master antisocial impulses we need to give them the skills to be able to do this.

Why is it so hard for children to control themselves?

Self-control is not traditionally part of a child's job description, but over the past 20 years scientists have gathered a lot more information about why children are particularly prone to failures of self-control compared with adults.

Let me introduce Ben. Ben tends to do whatever comes into his head, apparently without pausing to think about the impact or consequences of his actions. Emotionally unpredictable, Ben's behaviour is often atrocious – so bad in fact that going out with him in public can be a nightmare. Ben couldn't care less. His family says that he seems to have no 'off' button. His manners are non-existent, he has the attention span of a gnat and his reckless, confrontational behaviour means he is constantly getting himself into trouble. Ben displays a total disregard for rules and regulations and often comes across as selfish, boastful and immature.

Ben cuts an unattractive figure. We have all come across children who behave like Ben and, if we are honest, at times we can recognize elements of Ben in even the most immaculately-behaved child. Ben, however, is not a child. He is a 45-year-old adult and, prior to a road accident eight months ago, his personality and behaviour were very different. He was a gentle, shy, cultivated man much loved by his friends and respected by his work colleagues. Ben suffers from a condition called 'orbito-frontal syndrome', a pattern of disinhibited emotion and behaviour caused by damage to a particular part of his brain.

Cases of brain injury such as Ben's have provided researchers with invaluable insights into how the brain works and have been enormously helpful in mapping how different areas of the brain relate to specific abilities. Interestingly, what neuroscientists have also discovered is that the area of the brain damaged in Ben's case does not fully develop in perfectly normal human beings until well into their teenage years.

In the language of cognitive psychology, the prefrontal cortex is the command centre for the 'cool system'. This is the counterpart of – you guessed it – the 'hot system' and it seems that our ability to exercise effective self-control depends upon the way these two systems interact.

The 'hot system' is designed to produce rapid, automatic reactions to aspects of the environment to which we need to be attracted or by which it makes sense for us to be repelled. The hot system fires up almost instantaneously and dominates in situations where we find ourselves 'acting on the spur of the moment' or responding to 'gut instinct'. Sometimes called the 'emotional' brain, the hot system drives the sort of primal instincts that helped our ancestors find food and mates and avoid predators. It can rapidly create powerful states of arousal that encourage us to approach or avoid relevant hot spot stimuli. Physically, the control centre for the hot system seems to be located in the amygdala, a small almond-shaped area in the primitive forebrain.

By contrast the cool system gives us our ability to process more complex aspects of the world. The cool system is rational, logical and trades in the currency of information rather than high-octane emotion. With help from the intricate switchboard of the hippocampus and the frontal lobes, the cool system enables us to reflect on experience, analyse it and generate new strategies for moving forward.

Although functionally distinct, these two systems are linked. It is thought that neural connections wire up various hot spots and cool nodes within the brain. This web of connections gives the cool system the power to de-activate hot spots when appropriate. When temptation strikes and we fight off the urge to have a cigarette by reminding ourselves of the health risks, deliberately distracting ourselves or putting into place a contingency plan, we are using cooling strategies to damp down a hot system stimulus.

In children the cooling system takes time to evolve. The lower number of cool nodes, and poor connections with the relevant hot spots, tends to leave children at the mercy of their 'hot system' impulses.

Whilst I am not trying to suggest that all children are brain damaged, up into his teens even a perfectly normal child has neurological limitations that show up on a scan. These correspond with psychological limitations with which you may be all too familiar.

During adolescence, a time when the brain overall actually prunes back millions of redundant neural pathways, in the prefrontal cortex the density of neural branching actually becomes richer and more elaborate. This is significant because of the role that the prefrontal cortex plays in impulse control and decision making. One implication could be that we need to be providing appropriate challenges to stimulate this process of development. However, the key point is that the prefrontal cortex of the human brain, the seat of the cooling system, is simply not fully formed until adulthood. As a result it does not always work that efficiently in younger children.

So next time you are presented with a histrionic

outburst, unbearable moodiness, mad-cap risk taking or an infantile tantrum, take a deep breath. Before you condemn yourself as a terrible parent or your child as the spawn of Satan, spare a thought for the role played by biological timetabling.

> The rational cooling system in the brain takes time to evolve and isn't properly developed until adulthood.

A system under strain

When it comes to self-regulation it's not just the neural hardware in children's brains that is overdue for an upgrade; the same is true of the software. As we grow older more and more of what we do becomes a matter of habit. When you stop to think about it, even apparently simple tasks like brushing your teeth involve miraculous feats of co-ordination and perceptual judgement. When we learn a new skill the process of acquisition is time-consuming and effortful. Anyone who doubts this has only to witness the furrowed concentration on a young child's face as he begins to form clumsy letters with a pencil or the focus required by a toddler as she takes her first faltering steps.

In time, tasks that demand such conscious expenditure of mental energy in the early stages become automatic and effortless. The brain creates efficient protocols for walking, for writing, for riding a bicycle that fortunately mean such activities largely take care of themselves. Once learned, these tasks no longer drain the mind's resources as they did to begin with and what is freed up can be channelled towards other goals. Soon you can ride a bike and simultaneously plan what you are going to have for dinner. Ask a pre-schooler what he wants for tea during his initial outing on two wheels and he will most likely end up in the hedge.

The fact is that the brain's processing power, and in particular our capacity to devote conscious attention to things, is a finite resource. As adults we benefit from having already automated many aspects of our lives to the extent that we can depend on unconscious subroutines to deal fairly reliably with the everyday stuff (although from time to time we may still discover our toothbrush primed with moisturizer or our wallet in the fridge). Children, by contrast, are still assimilating many of the skills we take for granted. This means that on a day-to-day basis their concentration is being taxed to a much greater degree just by the routine business of daily life.

The reason this is so relevant when thinking about children's misbehaviour is that the regions of the brain involved in so-called 'executive functions' such as planning, solving complex problems, evaluating choices and switching between activities are precisely the same ones that enable us to inhibit impulses and regulate our feelings. This means that mental tasks involving a lot of processing power, even in seemingly unrelated domains, may have a knock-on effect on children's ability to keep their behaviour in check. Put simply, we need to understand that self-control is a form of mental labour. If mental effort is being expended in other directions there may not be enough gas left in the tank to fuel the engine of self-regulation.

Numerous times I have met parents deeply frustrated by

their child's ability to behave angelically at school while his conduct at home is running them ragged. Their argument runs: 'If he can manage to behave at school, why can't he do so at home?' There may of course be several explanations for this but, ironically, one factor may be that it is precisely *because* he is behaving well at school that he is coping less well at home. The exercise of self-control in one context may be using up available resources in the other. Sometimes when your child comes through the front door at the end of the school day she may already be running on empty.

Some interesting experimental evidence for the very real demands self-control places upon us has been provided by psychologist Roy Baumeister and colleagues. What Baumeister discovered was that if you take a group of people and encourage them to 'resist temptation' by sitting them near a plate of biscuits that they are forbidden to eat they will give up much more quickly on a later task involving copying complex figures. This was compared both to participants who had been allowed to eat the biscuits beforehand *and* a group who performed the experiment with no food present at all.

On the basis of his experiments Baumeister concluded that self-control is like a muscle. Exercising it within sensible limits increases its power, but like a muscle our self-control or 'self-regulatory strength' can also be pushed to the point of fatigue, resulting in a sudden and dramatic collapse. The way our new year's resolutions can so readily fall apart after a stressful day at work or we find ourselves drinking more than intended after 'holding it together' over the summer holidays offer everyday examples of the same phenomenon.

> Be aware that for children self-control is like a muscle. Exercising it makes it stronger but too much use and it gets tired.

The fact that the frontal lobes of the brain govern various different functions that all draw from the same mental pot suggests that if we can help increase the efficiency of some of those tasks, then we should be lightening the load on the prefrontal cortex as a whole. In theory this should make more resources available for other functions, including self-control. For example, if we help children become better at problem solving not only do we give them tools to handle situations in ways that are likely to create less stress for them, but we also release capacity to deal with any internal stress they have to tolerate.

If we are to help children master themselves we need to adopt a holistic approach that recognizes the way these different systems connect up and influence each other. One of the problems with using carrot and stick methods to target specific 'problem' behaviours is that they are often taken out of context. We can all too easily ignore the fact that children's ability to behave well is just one outcome of the mastery of several distinct but interrelated mental skills.

Where does this leave us?

Now you may be reading this thinking: 'Well, if there are all these legitimate biological reasons why my child struggles to control herself maybe I have no choice but to sit tight, grit my teeth, and wait for her brain to develop?'

On the contrary, the opposite is true. In the early 1970s

Walter Mischel took a group of 4 year olds and offered them a choice: either they could have one marshmallow straight away or, if they waited until the experimenter came back into the room, they could have two. Even at four years of age, two thirds of children successfully resisted the immediate temptation of the sweet in front of them. Even while their brains are not fully mature, many of these children *were* demonstrating a measure of self-control. There would seem absolutely no reason why this potential cannot be nurtured, just like any other innate ability. After all, we don't abandon teaching children to read in pre-school because they can't hope to read with the fluency they will have attained in a few years' time. Just like literacy, the development of self-control requires sustained input, support and stimulation.

Particularly encouraging is the fact that many of the children who managed to hold out in Mischel's experiment were observed using basic cooling strategies like distraction and talking to themselves. This raises the intriguing possibility that the children who successfully resisted temptation were not blessed with superior will-power, but simply had better tactics for handling such dilemmas. It could be argued that it is precisely during the period while their brains are still maturing that children can most benefit from being given practical strategies to compensate for their biological shortcomings.

What is most remarkable of all is how powerfully predictive the 'one-sweet-now' trial proved to be for the children who took part. Then, 12 to 14 years later, when the children from the original experiment were followed up, Mischel and his colleagues found that the 'resisters' were significantly outperforming the 'yielders' on a whole range of different measures. Those who had been able to wait were scoring as better adjusted, academically smarter and more resourceful. Those who had been unable to delay gratification were more introverted, had lower self-esteem, were more temperamental and demonstrably less able to cope under pressure.

What these results underline is not only how fundamentally self-control contributes to all manner of desirable skills and attributes, but also how crucial it is that this capacity is nurtured during children's formative years. I know from clinical experience that cooling strategies can be taught – and that they do make a difference. In the pages that follow I hope to introduce ways in which you can support and promote your child's emerging self-control skills in practical ways.

2
Developing supersenses

The ABC of feelings

It is past midnight on a dank, misty evening. You are standing on one end of what you thought was a deserted platform in an unfamiliar town waiting for a train. Because of the fog your visibility is limited. Your infant's pushchair is at your side. There is no sign of your train. Gradually you become aware of the steady fall of footsteps coming towards you. How do you react?

By now you are almost certainly in a state of heightened arousal. You probably feel uneasy. Your pupils have dilated and your senses become heightened as you scan instinctively for visual or auditory cues that might help you assess the possible threat. Automatically your respiratory rate has increased and oxygenated blood is diverted to your muscles and brain as your body readies itself for action.

However, you are not the only one scanning for information about an uncertain situation. The infant by your side is also staring intently. But he is not peering into the gloom trying to identify the shadowy stranger. Instead his gaze is fixed on you. He is searching for clues to his fate in the configuration of the 42 facial muscles that you use to register emotion. Depending upon what he finds in your expression, your child will either relax or become increasingly agitated.

When presented with an ambiguous or unfamiliar situation, the first place that most infants look for further information is in the faces of their caregivers. This process is called referencing. Children do this instinctively because from a very young age, even though they lack the ability to assess complex situations themselves, they have already become adept at reading the emotions on people's faces.

The American writer, poet and activist Audre Lord has claimed that 'our feelings are the most genuine path to knowledge' but for a child they are one of the few pathways open to him. Consequently he is highly reliant upon them. Long before his powers of reason mature, it is a child's untutored feelings that shepherd him through his period of greatest vulnerability. It is his emotions that prompt him to seek food and comfort and his emotions that keep him close to the adult carers upon whom he relies. Moreover it is the child's emotions that alert others to his needs. His sensitivity to the feelings of others also provides him with critical data about his immediate environment.

When your baby smiles back in response to your smile she is not simply imitating your behaviour. Rather the human brain appears to be equipped with specialized hardware that enables children to tap directly into the emotions they witness around them. How is this possible? Our knowledge has been recently advanced by the discovery of clusters of specialized brain cells known as 'mirror neurons'.

I feel what you feel

In Parma during the 1990s a research group led by neurologist Giacomo Rizzolatti made an astonishing discovery. They found that when macaque monkeys watch other monkeys grasping objects, certain regions of their brains involved in motor co-ordination begin firing *just as if the spectators themselves were performing the actions*. This is a remarkable thing. In response to a scatter of visual stimuli hitting the retina, via a mind-boggling feat of translation, similar patterns of activity were occurring almost instantaneously in specific brain centres within both the doer and the observer. Put simply: these mirror neurons seemed to be helping these monkeys to get inside each other's heads. In some senses both the performer and the observer were sharing the same experience, even though only one of them was actively taking part.

From an evolutionary point of view this is a fantastically useful development. It allows us to update existing skills and prepare for the acquisition of new ones simply by watching others. We see a professional dancer gliding across the floor and we instantly have an intuitive sense of what the movement would feel like – even if most of us would be hard pushed to replicate the motion with our own bodies!

Some scientists have argued that it is the ability of higher primates to 'participate' by watching in this way that has given *homo sapiens* such a leg up the evolutionary ladder. It presumably also explains why spectating, whether in sporting arenas or theatres, can engage us like it does. We don't simply watch the star striker putting away that winning goal: in our heads we are there on the pitch, adrenaline coursing through our systems, our muscles unconsciously twitching as we anticipate the thwack of boot against ball.

Other researchers have found compelling evidence that the neural mirroring process may also support the transmission of certain emotions. It seems likely that such cells create an empathic bridge that gives us direct access to what another person is feeling by actually recreating aspects of the emotion inside the observer.

For example, if you look at the brain of someone experiencing the emotion of disgust on an MRI scanner, an area of the brain called the anterior insula lights up. However, if the same person just watches someone else pulling an expression of disgust, the anterior insula reacts in much the same way. A resonance of disgust is recreated inside the brain of the observer. When we see an expression on someone's face we not only recognize what they are feeling but experience an echo of that feeling ourselves.

Is it catching?

The fact that this appears to be an innate hard-wired capacity, rather than just a skill that is developed, means that children are just as susceptible to emotional priming as adults. There are over 200 words in the English language to describe our different emotions, suggesting that there are many different shades and hues of emotional experience. However, at the core of our emotional lives there appear to be six basic emotions (happiness, surprise, fear, sadness, disgust and anger). These core feelings correspond to virtually identical facial expressions throughout the world, regardless of local culture and tradition.

Studies of young babies suggest that from a very early age infants recognize and respond to basic emotional cues on the faces of their carers. The mirror neuron research implies that babies in facial recognition trials are not just imitating what they see in front of them but are, to at least some degree, experiencing first-hand the emotions with which they are presented. When we frown at our children they feel the chill of displeasure; when we smile and laugh we flood them with the sunlight of their own capacity for joy.

> Your children feel what you feel. They learn their response from your response. Help rehearse them in experiencing positive emotions.

We have always instinctively understood that emotions are contagious, but neuroscience is giving us new insights into how and why. What this research does suggest is that we need to take seriously the responsibility of monitoring the emotional climate to which our children are exposed. Just as over time a persistent trickle of water will carve out a channel for itself, whenever we display an emotion we are most likely priming, rehearsing and reinforcing a bias towards the same emotional responses in our children. What they see, they not only imitate, but probably learn to feel too.

Becoming an emotional coach

Before we get too anxious about the negative impact that our own moods might be having on our children, it is important to recognize the very positive opportunities that this amazing human faculty also provides. Because we can use our faces, voices and bodies to trigger them, we can introduce children to their own emotions in a relatively controlled fashion. More importantly, we can also use our own emotional reactions to conduct young children through emotional transitions they will later need to master themselves.

Ellie is a spirited toddler due to attend her friend Maisie's birthday party later in the afternoon. Throughout the morning she has been whipping herself up into a state of manic excitement. She is currently discharging her mounting internal pressure by dancing around the sitting room and jumping off the furniture. Predictably the only consequence of this behaviour is to cause her levels of excitement and arousal to escalate further.

Because the mirroring process works both ways, her mother Jenny is now also experiencing a corresponding level of agitation (and not just because she cannot face the prospect of washing the sofa cushions). Under such circumstances Jenny would, of course, be forgiven for seeking to relieve her own tension by 'losing her rag' and yelling at her daughter.

However, instructing a child to 'calm down' while you remain in a state of high arousal yourself presents the infant with a confusing double-message. The words demand one response, but if Jenny pursues this strategy the cues from her agitated body language are likely to have the opposite effect in her daughter, maintaining Ellie's rocketing arousal levels. To evoke a calmer mood in Ellie, Jenny will need to transmit behaviour cues likely to elicit the desired mood. This means that Jenny must either (a) convincingly disguise what she is really feeling or (b) take herself out of the situation until she can get into a more relaxed state herself before tackling her daughter.

> Show the change you want to see in your child. There's no point in telling a child to calm down if you are agitated yourself. You need to calm down first so your child can see how it is done.

Ellie needs help because she is little. As yet she lacks the capacity to regulate her reserves of nervous energy. But what she can be given is an experience of 'coming down' through exposure to adult behavioural cues aimed at inducing a calmer state of mind. Automatically picking up on her mother's non-verbal triggers, the mirroring process should mean that Ellie will feel her own tension beginning to dissipate.

When dealing with children's behaviour, research underlines that our non-verbal communications matter just as much as the content of what we are saying. If Jenny is successful then Ellie will at least start to get a sense of what the transition out of a highly aroused state feels like. She may not be able to replicate it on her own as yet, but at least she will have another example in her repertoire to draw upon when she needs to make such a shift on her own.

If we want children to learn to regulate their own emotions it is really important that there is consistency between the emotions we describe in words and the non-verbal cues that we attach to those descriptions. Otherwise we can be talking about one feeling while unconsciously generating something very different in our children. This ends up weakening the associations between the labels we provide and the feeling states we are trying to map onto them. Because the strength of these associations is crucial to giving the rational, thinking brain purchase upon the primitive feeling brain this really does matter. When our words and our feelings become dislocated from one another we leave ourselves at the mercy of our emotions.

> Make sure your words match your body language and behaviour. If you say 'calm' you need to show 'calm'.

Learning to label emotions

In order to regulate their emotions it stands to reason that children first need to know what it is they *are* feeling. They must also be able to separate themselves out from the experience of feeling so they can see what's happening to them. This is the difference between allowing yourself to be carried along in the current of a powerful river and finding a secure position on the bank from which to observe the seething waters in front of you. In order to process experience, the thinking brain needs to translate it into terms that it can deal with.

On most undergraduate psychology courses students are introduced to the notion that the Inuit people have many different words for types of snow whereas in English we have only one. The example is used to illustrate the inter-relationship between thought, perception and language.

The idea is that because the Inuit people have more snow-related vocabulary they also experience whole dimensions of snow of which we westerners are unaware: our poverty of words and concepts in this area restricts what we can see. To us snow is just snow. Our lack of language leaves us unattuned to the more subtle distinctions that an Eskimo might discern between *aput* ('snow on the ground') and *piqsirpoq* ('drifting snow'). Unlike our Inuit cousins we are partially 'snow-blind'.

This is the basis of the imposingly entitled 'Sapir–Whorf linguistic hypothesis': that what we *can* think depends upon the availability of the appropriate words to help us think it. Ironically, it turns out that the Inuit snow vocabulary has been somewhat overplayed. By 1978 the seven words for snow that Benjamin Whorf mentions in his

1940s article had mysteriously reached 50 thanks to the exaggeration of later writers. By 1984 the *New York Times* was referring to 100 different terms!

While this famous example no longer packs quite the same punch and linguists and philosophers now question whether vocabulary alone determines what we can think, at the heart of Sapir and Whorf's theory there remains a valid principle. Our children do require a reliable emotional vocabulary if they are to make meaningful distinctions between feeling states, and develop workable strategies to manage them.

> Children need to learn words for what they are feeling.

It is striking that in our culture the first features of the world we label for children usually relate to properties of the physical world. Shapes and colours, numbers and animals, and different forms of transport monopolize the toys and books designed for very young children.

Clearly a child needs to be able to distinguish between red and yellow or a cow and a duck, and strong contrasts will always excite children's interest. However, it is telling that in a society that struggles with the consequences of children's emotions, we often wait so long before we help them label their own feelings and those of others.

This may be because feelings seem a bit abstract and therefore potentially hard for a child to grasp, but in fact natural selection has already sensitized children to the emotional undercurrents of the world around them. However, if they are not to be overwhelmed by the constant turmoil of feelings inside, children need to be able to organize and classify their emotional reactions. Giving them labels is an important start. Not only does the act of naming a feeling involve stepping back from it, thereby reducing its immediate intensity, but it leaves children in a position to start grouping and analysing their emotional experiences. The human brain is remarkably good at searching for patterns. A reliable label will begin to clarify the circumstances under which the feeling in question occurs, and ultimately help your child decide which strategies are appropriate for dealing with it.

The A to Z of emotions

In the light of this it is important that in the early years children are given all the help they can to become emotionally literate. You can do this in a number of ways. Firstly, make an effort to attach appropriate verbal flags to your own feelings. When you are aware that your face and body are communicating an emotion give it a name. Tell your child when you are feeling happy, sad, excited, confused or playful.

For the reasons discussed above, try not to expose your children to too much of your negative emotion. Having said that, since feelings like fear, anger and frustration need the most stringent management, being able to discern and identify such emotions is especially important. When you locate feelings of anger or distress using words you demystify them and transform these states into mental objects that can be confronted and tackled. You are taking the first steps in helping your child tame the beast.

> Tell your child how *you* feel to help her put a name to her emotions.

You can also help your child map out her emotional landscape by providing a commentary on the emotions that you observe your child experiencing. This needs to be done sensitively. If you misjudge a feeling state or are too quick to impose your own assumptions without reading your child's cues accurately you may confuse matters. However, remarking that Toby 'looks like a really happy and proud boy' when he approaches you beaming with his latest paint-splattered masterpiece is unlikely to be far off the mark. Similarly, commenting on Annie's 'sad face' before offering comfort and a plaster for her freshly grazed knee will begin to cement useful associations for her.

While it is a good idea to avoid making dogmatic statements about what a child *is* feeling, it is perfectly legitimate to comment upon the emotional signals that your child is sending out. Making the observation that your son or daughter 'seems cross' or 'looks cross' rather than pronouncing that he or she *is* cross may seem like a subtle distinction. However, the former is not only more respectful (just note how irritating you find it next time someone tells you what you are feeling ...) but the provisional nature of the observation invites the child to check out whether what is happening inside tallies with the message being sent out. Ultimately you want your child to be the foremost authority on the state of his own heart and mind. If you start taking that responsibility away from him at the outset of his life you may be setting an unhelpful precedent.

> Don't tell a child how he is feeling – but do encourage him to tell you by making observations: 'You look as if you are feeling cross.'

Picture this

The level of difficulty even older children encounter in distinguishing between their emotions can be surprising. By the time we become adults the distinctions seem self-evident, but this is not the case for a child whose mental experience is still largely unorganized. However, the basic hard-wired connections between facial expressions and emotional states can be easily recruited to help familiarize your child with different feelings.

You can help younger children with this task by getting hold of one of the commercially available sets of cards that depict a range of facial expressions. These present a variety of stylized emotions and can provide a useful aid for introducing your child to basic categories of feeling. Alternatively, you could simply cut out pictures from magazines. If you are feeling adventurous you can also use a digital camera to make your own customized 'emotional mug shots' featuring family and friends and, of course, your child. The process of making these can be just as informative for children as the finished items and the hapless gurning of family members as they attempt various expressions usually makes this an entertaining project for all involved.

> Use drawings or photos to discuss expressions and emotions.

Having a set of images available allows your child to move beyond the basic skill of identifying the different emotions. Children can be asked to pick out a card that represents the opposite of a target expression (happy as opposed to sad; calm as opposed to excited and so on) or to begin grouping feelings that frequently occur together. The cards can also prove a helpful aid as an accompaniment to stories. Your child can be asked to select expressions that correspond with the feelings a character might be experiencing in a particular situation: 'How do you think Pooh felt when he got stuck in Rabbit's house? Let's pick out some cards that show us how he might feel...' This kind of tactic will not only develop a child's ability to empathize with the feelings of others but also keep a child much more actively engaged.

Tell me a story

Whether or not you use expression cards as a prop, reading stories to your child is an important means of encouraging emotional literacy. The best loved children's stories always take a character on some form of emotional journey, usually encouraging some level of identification from the listener. Good story telling, like facial cues, evokes the emotions it describes. Discussing with your child the motivations, experience and reactions of major and minor characters is a painless and natural way to introduce her to a wide range of different emotional states. If the story is well written, the feelings depicted will relate to situations and events that your child can comprehend, making it possible for her to begin grasping the context of emotions and the circumstances likely to generate particular emotional reactions.

> Read to your child and discuss how characters might be feeling: 'Do you think he's feeling scared/cross/happy/upset?'

While it may look like similar opportunities are offered by films and television programmes, reading to your children has added value when it comes to promoting emotional literacy. There are a couple of reasons for this. For a start, children being read to have to do more of the mental work. They don't have the luxury of absorbing what they see in front of them. Instead the words that they read (or are read to them) are a code that has to be actively unlocked by the child's imagination. Your child must not only paint the picture in his mind's eye but is also required to colour it in using his own feelings.

More crucially, the act of reading connects up the thinking and feeling brain in a way that watching television often does not. Written words stimulate multiple areas of the brain, producing an emotional response within the limbic system, but also activating networks of meaning in the cortex. The 'cooling processes' that will ultimately allow your child to soothe his own distress or calm his own anger rely on the part of the mind that deals in words. Stories that fuse feelings and meanings lay the foundation for personal control.

All mixed up

Me: So what are your feelings saying to you at the moment, Lisa?

[Lisa says nothing but twists her hair between grubby fingers.]

Me: Okay, maybe that's too hard a question to answer right now.

[Lisa stares sullenly out of the window and says nothing.]

Me: Maybe we could talk a bit about your picture. This girl here in the beautiful green dress . . . Is she pleased to be with her friends or not? I am finding it quite hard to tell from the look on her face.

Lisa: I call her 'Spaghetti Girl'. She's stupid.

Me: What an interesting name. Why is she called 'Spaghetti Girl'?

Lisa: Because that's what she's like. Everything inside her is all squirmy and wormy and mixed up together.

Me: That sounds pretty messy – having everything jumbled up inside like that . . .

Lisa: [conspiratorially] Sometimes she wears a green dress. And sometimes she wears a red dress. And sometimes she wears a blue dress. And sometimes . . . sometimes . . . sometimes . . .

Me: Yes?

Lisa: Sometimes that silly Spaghetti Girl wears all her dresses at once. And she gets *very* hot! [giggles]

This session with a 6-year-old girl provided a telling insight into her emotional world. Lisa (not her real name) had plenty of reason to feel mixed up like the girl in her picture. Her mother was struggling with a serious alcohol addiction, and could switch very rapidly from being kind and caring at one moment, to becoming angry, aggressive or withdrawn the next. Lisa never knew what she would find when she came home from school. She could be baking by her mum's side, or hiding behind a closed bedroom door while her mother ranted and raged in the corridor.

Lisa had done what many children in such difficult circumstances do: she had taken her negative feelings about her unreliable carer and turned them in on herself to become the 'stupid' Spaghetti Girl in her picture. However, although this exchange reflected a level of disturbance in Lisa's internal world, it also represented an important step forward. What Lisa was exploring was the notion that a person can feel more than one emotion at the same time.

The different coloured dresses worn by the unfortunate, mixed-up Spaghetti Girl stood both for the changeable nature of her mother and also the painful cocktail of conflicting feelings that Lisa held about her. She loved her mother but also feared her. She idolized her but secretly despised her behaviour when she had been drinking. The fact that it was perfectly normal to hold such conflicting feelings about someone simultaneously was a revelation to Lisa. Like many children she had assumed that feelings about things and people should be consistent and that she ought to feel one emotion at a time.

What Lisa gradually realized is that it is possible, and indeed perfectly normal, to experience a whole range of very different feelings about the same person. Even more importantly, she began to grasp that these contrasting feelings can coexist. Being able to separate out and identify her different strands of feeling helped her impose some sort of order upon the noisy chaos of her internal world and feel less at the mercy of her emotions.

Although her case was extreme, some of Lisa's misconceptions about her feelings are commonplace amongst children. As your child grows older it is helpful to introduce the idea that it is possible to hold many feelings simultaneously and that our feelings are often jumbled up together, sometimes making it hard to know what is going on inside us.

> Help your child to understand you can be angry with somebody but still love them – it is possible to have more than one feeling at the same time.

An analogy helpful to some children is that identifying feelings is rather like learning to tune into the different instruments in an orchestra. To demonstrate how this is done you could do worse than listen with your child to the famous recording of Prokofiev's *Peter and the Wolf* in which the narrator introduces each of the instruments in the orchestra in turn, demonstrating how each instrument carries the signature theme of an animal in the story.

Buried feelings – beware!

It is also worth explaining to school-age children that sometimes our feelings do not want to be put in the spotlight. Sigmund Freud's greatest insight was that it is our hidden feelings, the ones of which we are least aware, that can often have the most impact on our choices and behaviour. In Freud's model of the human mind many mental health problems result from the strain of stuffing painful or incongruent feelings below the level of consciousness. The enterprise of psychoanalysis aims to bring these submerged feelings into the light of day. By learning to acknowledge and tolerate the hidden fantasies and emotions that previously felt so alarming, Freud and his followers believed that the damaging build-up of mental pressure could be released. Freud viewed this process as fundamental to our emotional well-being.

It is certainly true that repressed feelings can cause difficulties for adults and children alike. Studies of particularly resilient children – those who deal well with life's setbacks – indicate that not only are they more able to articulate what they are feeling but tend to be much more at ease with the full range of their emotions. They are able to acknowledge 'difficult' feelings that other children find threatening.

In order for your child to feel confident about facing rather than evading his more disturbing emotions it is necessary for you to give several clear messages.

Firstly, you must let him know that *no one is responsible for what they feel*. Our emotions are usually an automatic, gut response to a person or situation. It therefore makes no sense to blame someone for experiencing any kind of feeling, even a highly antisocial one. When your nine-year-old tells you he wants to rip the head off the little brother who has just tipped his football card collection on the floor there is no point reprimanding him or telling him he doesn't. Judging from the look in his eye he really does! He is giving you (and himself) a very candid snapshot of what his emotions are telling him at that precise moment. Thankfully, this is not to say they won't change.

Because we are not responsible for the feelings we experience, teach your child that she doesn't have to censor her emotions. In fact we give emotions less power over us when we acknowledge them honestly. Denying feelings usually only makes them stronger. We may have to curb the way in which children *express* their feelings, especially if they start violating the boundaries of acceptable behaviour (swearing at us or being deliberately offensive for example). However, we must also give our children permission to hate, loathe and despise us at times

– however hard that can be for us, or however unjust it may feel.

In order for children to feel comfortable about not shutting off their feelings the distinction must also be made – even to very young children – between *having* a feeling and *acting* on it. The message you need to broadcast repeatedly is that the urge to subject one's sibling to a slow and painful death is both natural and acceptable. Nevertheless, any action based on that desire is definitely not.

> Tell your child that it's OK to feel whatever it is they feel ... but it isn't always OK to act on that feeling.

This can be a surprisingly difficult distinction for even older children to grasp. Even into their early teens children will plead the defence of 'provocation'. When a child tells you 'She was winding me up so I hit her,' he may as well be telling you, 'I released the ball so it fell to the ground.' In a child's mind the emotional state induced (frustration) and the way it is expressed (violence) can become so closely identified that he loses any sense of ever having had a choice about his response. According to the magical thinking of children, feelings can actually make things happen. In your son's mind his sister may as well have slapped herself round the face once she started down the path of aggravation. The more your child is able to register and identify feelings, building the detachment required to become their steward rather than their slave, the more choice he will have about how he responds to his emotions.

The shutting off of problematic feelings appears to be second-nature for young children, and they often need patient encouragement if they are to be schooled in less-clumsy ways of handling things and learn to tolerate feelings that make them feel uncomfortable or anxious.

Newton's third law of motion states that 'for every action there is an equal and opposite reaction'. This is largely true of our feelings, which also tend to coexist in tension with their opposites. However, as the example of 'Spaghetti Girl' Lisa reminds us, a child can find such contradictions especially hard to tolerate.

Children often respond by attempting to dispose of the feeling they do not want by repressing it. The child psychotherapist Melanie Klein argued that children learn to do this very early on in order to preserve an idealized mental model of the person who cares for them. This is because they cannot afford to risk being dependent upon a mother or father who might let them down, even though sometimes this is unavoidable. Like Lisa they try and bury the unwanted 'bad' mother in their unconscious and hold on to the 'good' one. Only in adolescence do most children feel robust enough to start dealing with their parents as real people, warts and all, whose imperfections no longer feel quite so dangerous. The free use of such primitive defences does, however, leave children particularly vulnerable to characteristic swings of feeling and attachment.

Getting the feelings out

Danny and Mike have been friends since playgroup. Most of the time they are very happy in each other's company but today there has been a serious falling-out. Mike has returned home from school in tears vehemently declaring that he *hates* Danny and that he *never* wants to see him again. In the post-mortem that follows it becomes clear that Danny's transgression has been a pretty minor one: he failed to bring in the action figure that he had promised for Mike to play with. But Mike will not be consoled. He is incandescent with fury.

There is a Russian Orthodox saying that 'the greatest virtues cast the longest shadows' and ironically Mike and Danny's relationship has fallen prey to the very strategy that until now has ensured its success. Because Danny and Mike relied totally upon each other in the initially alien world of playgroup they both worked hard to preserve an idealized vision of their friendship.

Danny had unconsciously suppressed his irritation when Mike regularly used to invade his personal space and get a bit physical when they were playing together. Mike chose to 'ignore' how angry he had felt every time Danny used to take his special toys off the shelf when he came round to his house.

Although these two friends genuinely care for each other, under the surface unacknowledged resentments have been ticking away like a time bomb. Today the balance was accidentally tipped. Danny's moment of forgetfulness unwittingly unleashed years of buried resentment. This is why Mike now finds himself in the grip of such dispropor-tionate fury.

Mike has fallen prey to what Freud called 'the return of the repressed'. If this occurs in the wrong way at the wrong time the consequences can be devastating. Repressed material does have a horrible habit of returning – often when we are stressed or least equipped to cope with it – and, because they rely on basic emotional strategies like denial and repression, children are particularly prone to triggering it. Although their friendship will be saved and the row eventually forgotten, it would have been better for both children if their latent irritation could have been identified and dealt with at the time. Unfortunately, neither child had developed the skills to do this.

When his mother used to observe Mike tensing up each time Danny took his sacred toys down from the shelf she had often told her son to 'play nicely' and reminded him that it was part of being a good friend to share his toys. True enough, but it might have helped Mike if, once Danny had gone, his mother had observed that 'it can feel quite hard when someone plays with your special things without asking ...' This would have allowed Mike to validate his feelings of resentment and prevented the toxic build-up of repressed emotion that nearly destroyed their friendship.

If you notice a child being irritated or tense or annoyed by the actions of somebody else (especially somebody they love) help them express those feelings rather than repressing them.

Heart to heart: the importance of empathy

Mike and Danny's friendship was jeopardized by the accumulation of petty, unacknowledged resentments. However, the ultimate source of the problem was a repeated breach of empathy on both sides – Danny's indifference to Mike's feelings about his toys and Mike's insensitivity to his guest's needs and desires.

The actress Meryl Streep, whose uncanny ability to inhabit the emotional lives of other people brought her

Oscar-winning acclaim, once commented that the power of empathy is 'the great gift of human beings'. From a psychological perspective she is completely right: empathy is not just a moral virtue, it is also the most effective brake on children's bad behaviour. Our ability to put ourselves into the shoes of others and attune ourselves sympathetically with their experience has been shown to help us clamp down on our more antisocial instincts.

Experimental findings offer increasing support for the view of the 18th century German philosopher, Arthur Schopenhauer, who concluded that 'compassion is the basis of all morality'. Ultimately, we want our children to behave because they appreciate the effects of their actions on other people. We don't want them not to bully, cheat and steal because of the trouble they could get into, or even because subduing such urges wins them stickers, praise or adulation. Deep down we want children who avoid these things because they know they cause suffering to others.

Studies have actually demonstrated that fostering empathy skills is more likely to produce enduring pro-social behaviour than punishments or bribes for good behaviour. One researcher found that children rewarded for behaving well became so dependent on the rewards themselves that when they were withdrawn their behaviour got worse. At the other end of the scale, criminals classified as sociopathic are amongst the most dangerous precisely because their lack of feeling for their fellow human beings makes them capable of almost anything. The message of the available research is this: if you want your child to be able to control his behaviour you should do all you can to help him become more empathetic.

> Encourage your child to be sensitive to the needs and
> feelings of others. 'If you do this, how will he feel?'

Encouragingly, all the research evidence points to a strong link between children's capacity for empathy and their powers of self-control. Research has shown that children who score highly on impulse control measures are also more likely to demonstrate pro-social and empathic behaviours.

Just because such a relationship exists between two factors does not, of course, mean one has caused the other. Even if this was so, we have no way of knowing which is causing which. Maybe these children were more empathic *because* they had better levels of self-control, rather than the other way round?

In fact this might well be the case. Children who are better able to regulate their own emotional arousal may be better equipped to 'tune into' others without becoming emotionally overwhelmed by their own responses. On the other hand, we know that children and young adults who are given empathy training do start behaving more considerately towards others, a result that suggests becoming more empathic does indeed enhance your powers of self-control in some situations.

The most likely explanation is that the two may be complementary: understanding that our actions might cause someone else pain gives you more motivation to hold back. Meanwhile, the ability to control your own emotions may put you in a better position to engage with other people's feelings.

You may also be interested to know that time and again children who score highly on empathy also tend to do better academically. As Professor Delores Gallo, the educationalist, has noted: 'It is not just moral reasoning but reasoning generally which benefits from empathic understanding.' This may be because some of the skills related to empathy – including emotional regulation, perspective taking, flexibility of thought and a capacity for reflection – also support learning ability. Whatever the connection, it gives all parents yet another good reason to nurture empathy.

The expanding heart

Some of the building blocks of empathy are laid at birth. We have already looked at the remarkable inbuilt ability of even very young infants to attune themselves to the emotions of those around them. You will no doubt have encountered for yourself situations in which toddlers become infected with the feelings of their peers. When a young infant falls over and cries you can bet that before long other toddlers around her will also be bawling. In fact, when one year olds were shown videotapes of crying children most of them began showing signs of distress themselves, furrowing their brows, sticking their lips out and sucking anxiously on their hands, their clothing or a comforting toy. But is this really empathy in the true sense of the word? Instinctive mirroring may enable babies to replicate something of what others are feeling, but surely this is different from being able to appreciate the significance of those feelings for another person?

Around a child's first birthday a significant change begins to take place. In a research project in which mothers were trained to spot and record empathic responses from their children, by 13 to 15 months more than half the children in the study showed signs of trying hug or pat their mothers when they showed distress. By 20 months their empathic behaviours were becoming more sophisticated. The infants were bringing blankets, soft toys and bandages to comfort their mothers, and even asking them if they were okay. By their second birthdays empathic overtures were being extended to a wider circle, even including strangers.

Between 2 and 3 years of age children become increasingly adept at spotting situations where others are upset and offering support. They can be found helping re-build fallen towers, replacing broken crayons and even spontaneously bringing plasters for bleeding fingers. Between the ages of 6 and 8 advances in children's cognitive abilities have put another vital piece in place. From this age children are capable of proper perspective taking. In other words they are not only able to appreciate what someone else is feeling but better able to understand *why* they are feeling it. They have learned to see the situation through someone else's eyes.

Understanding just how early on children are able to demonstrate empathy means that almost from birth parents have a useful window of opportunity to nurture their child's empathy potential. As the educationalist Charles Flatter reminds us: 'Children come into the world predisposed to empathize with the feelings of other people but seem to lose the capacity if they are not encouraged to develop it.' Unless we recognize how early on children's capacity for empathy develops we are unlikely to nurture it properly.

So what can parents do to support the growth of this most precious human talent? Well, the growing body of research into this area has given us some clear pointers. As with all skills we want children to master, one of the keys is to demonstrate those skills ourselves so they can follow our lead. If our children have not felt understood it is going to be hard for them to extend understanding to others. For most children their relationship with you will give them a template to imitate and reinforce for them the value of empathic engagement.

> Show children how *you* are sensitive to the needs and feelings of others at every opportunity.

Strengthening the bond between you

The early months of a baby's life are often a master-class in empathic responsiveness. When you watch skilfully attuned mothers with their children, the interaction between them resembles a playful dance in which both parties seamlessly anticipate and respond to the actions of each other. The baby experimentally waves a toy in front of her own face, eyes widening in surprise; her mother responds by making an exaggerated expression of surprise of her own and simultaneously making soothing, cooing noises and maybe reaching out with a reassuring touch. The baby gurgles with pleasure and her mother responds by telling her in a lilting, sing-song voice that she is 'such a clever girl'. And so it goes on.

Mothers who become adept at reading their baby's communications can tell what she needs and when – whether it be a feed, a sleep or a change of nappy – almost before the child consciously knows herself. But, just as importantly, the baby learns to view the mother as someone who understands and anticipates her needs. This is her first experience of empathy and it is a formative one.

One of the difficulties for mothers unfortunate enough to suffer from postnatal depression is that the relaxed rhythm of this formative dance between mother and child can be disrupted. Various studies have shown that a sustained breach of empathy in the early months can have some consequences for a child's emotional, cognitive and social development in the early years. However, it is reassuring that such differences tend to work themselves out as children mature, given a supportive environment. The human brain is a remarkably plastic and adaptable organ. This means that we can keep on learning. When it comes to empathy training it is rarely too late.

As your child grows older, his schooling in empathy will depend increasingly on your ability to listen to him. It is very easy for parents to feel like air traffic controllers as they juggle the multiple demands of co-ordinating their children's school, social and family commitments. Under such circumstances many of us fall into a directive, business-like or even militaristic style of interacting with our kids – issuing our orders, demanding constant updates as to whether they have remembered their gym kit, done their history project or written that thank-you letter. Life can feel enormously busy, and under the weight of this pressure 'conversations' with our children can easily degenerate into a stream of commands and instructions. I know this only too well. Because you are so familiar with your children, it is easy to cut them off mid-flow or finish their thoughts and sentences for them. However, your child is unlikely to experience this as empathy – quite the opposite in fact.

> Make time to talk – and listen – every day.

However busy things get, try and ensure that you still find time in your day during which you can talk properly to your child, and more importantly *listen* to what she has to say. Children who able to share their problems with their parents and discuss their feelings become more empathic towards others. But in order for this to happen you have to create a climate in which this is encouraged.

- Try and spend time together at a point in the day when both of you are likely to be relaxed. This might be just before bed or after tea, depending upon what fits best with your domestic routines.

- Rather than formally sitting your child down to 'have a conversation', try and develop a routine activity or ritual (like doing the crossword together with an older child) that provides a comfortable context in which such chats can take place. Boys, in particular, often prefer it if there is some notional joint task to take the spotlight off their feelings.

- During these times, learn to listen without interrupting or taking charge of the conversation. Always let your child finish what she has to say.

- While your child is talking, pay attention. Look interested and *be* interested. Don't assume that you know what they are getting at. Show your child you are actively listening by maintaining a good level of eye contact – usually about a third of the time as a rough guide – and using non-verbal signals like nodding or dropping in the occasional 'uh huh'. These cues tell your child that you regard what he has to tell you as important and that you are doing your best to pay attention.

- When your child has finished telling you something, offer a brief paraphrase of what she has said. This will demonstrate that you have been listening and underlines your desire to check you have properly understood your child's communication.

- Try and identify any implicit emotions in what your child is saying. 'I imagine it must have really hurt your feelings when Justin said that to you...' Speculate rather than pronounce, but rest secure in the knowledge that when you get it right you will be strengthening the empathic bond between you.

By developing your own listening skills not only will you help your child feel understood and improve your relationship, but you will also be modelling skills that your child will need in order to behave empathically towards others.

Getting the balance right

Some illuminating work has been done on the relationship between the development of empathy in the early years and the way in which parents express themselves. Several studies indicate that parents who demonstrate high levels of positive emotions through praise and enthusiasm are more likely to have children with high levels of empathy.

Psychologists suggest that by helping children to experience and express emotion, these high levels of positive feeling help children to become more at ease when it comes to experiencing other people's emotions.

The flip side of the coin is that if children are raised in a climate of intense negative emotion they may become over-aroused and experience real difficulties in learning about their own emotions, let alone those of others. Such children are unable to regulate their distressed feelings. They protect themselves by shutting off from others. Being met with threatening, rejecting or inconsistent treatment by caregivers appears to have a similar effect.

> By displaying positive emotions you are helping your child become more empathic towards others.

On the other hand it is not a good idea to wrap your infant in cotton wool and protect him from anything negative. Allowing your child to witness some level of distress in others can actually help foster empathic responding. The trick is not to expose your child to degrees of emotion (either negative or positive) that are too intense for him to handle. However, always try and ensure that the balance falls in favour of positive, upbeat, affirming emotions.

> Allow your child to see negative emotions, but in limited amounts. Don't let it become too intense – in either direction.

Fine-tuning the empathy response

In addition to creating an empathic environment at home there are some more direct ways in which you can nurture your child's empathic potential. The first is to notice and reinforce occasions when your son or daughter demonstrates empathy. When a child shows concern for someone else, your toddler attempts to console his howling playmate with an offer of a bedraggled soft toy, or your teenage daughter steps aside to let her friend have the last ticket to the gig, be on hand to affirm such behaviour with your praise and respect.

When a child does show empathy, and at those critical times when he doesn't, research indicates that it is a good idea to frame the incident in relation to his character rather than just his behaviour. Emphasize that your child has done a kind thing because he has a kind nature: that's the sort of boy he is. Similarly, when he fails to show empathy appropriately, express your surprise as well as your disappointment because you know he's 'not normally like that'. Researchers have found that strengthening the notion that empathy is part of your child's natural character is likely to engender more empathic conduct. The technical name for this process is 'positive trait attribution', which is a fancy way of saying that the more strongly you define someone in a certain way, the more likely they will be to act in line with that definition. However, do make sure your attributions are realistic and credible.

> Tell your child she is a kind and thoughtful person, and always comment on behaviour that supports this – or show surprise when it doesn't.

Discuss with your child how actions can influence feelings and prepare her for situations in which an empathic response will be required of her. Explain that Grandma will be feeling tired and sore after her operation. Help your daughter to think beforehand about what sort of behaviour might be appropriate under such circumstances. Getting your child to role play a situation from someone else's point of view has also proved a genuinely useful method for helping children extend their empathic understanding.

Studies with school-age children have shown that learning about examples of famously altruistic individuals like Mother Teresa, Albert Schweitzer or Martin Luther King can inspire children to cultivate their own powers of empathy.

> Tell your child about people who are heroes for kind behaviour as well as those famous for their exploits.

Also, help your child become proficient at reading and interpreting non-verbal 'body language'. Let them know that an open palm facing upwards is a sign of truth and honesty, that closed body language indicates that someone feels threatened, that a head slightly tilted to one side signals attention whereas a head thrust forward is more likely to convey aggression. As your children mature, train them to spot the non-verbal leakage that can so easily provide clues to people's real feelings. There are lots of books that can help you both get started and plenty of opportunity to practise honing your skills together.

> Have a shared project with your child to learn to read body language.

Finally, help your child to avoid prejudice and the breakdown of empathy by emphasizing what your child shares in common with people who may appear very different. Projects attempting to tackle racism in schools have found it helpful to begin by focusing on shared characteristics, traits and goals before highlighting racial or cultural features that distinguish a particular group or nationality. The same strategy applies when your child encounters someone who is disabled or whose sexual orientation may be different to his own. Help your child realize that what he shares in common with other people far transcends anything that might set them apart.

> Make sure you highlight similarities between people before discussing the differences.

When we react with prejudice empathy has already broken down. Prejudice always de-humanizes others, turning them into objects so we stop seeing them as people like ourselves. If the human race was better as sustaining empathy, our children would be growing up in a more tolerant, less war-torn world. Just like charity, empathy begins at home. The implications of raising empathic kids are more wide-reaching than just ensuring a more peaceful life for us as parents.

One final caveat: don't unwittingly perpetuate prejudice yourself by devoting more time to fostering empathy skills in your girls than in your boys. In western culture we tend to expect girls to be more empathic than boys and this can easily become a self-fulfilling prophecy. On almost every level, emotionally and cognitively girls do usually mature earlier than boys who on average – as far as I can gather – until their early teens only outstrip girls in tasks involving spatial navigation. (Yes, it's true: men are better at reading maps!) Boys are also more overtly aggressive than girls. For these reasons it is even more important to hone their powers of empathy. In terms of these skills boys are a vulnerable population: they really need your help.

Only connect

If any further motivation were needed, perhaps we should conclude by focusing on one of the main findings from the positive psychology researchers. Human happiness depends in a large measure on our ability to form meaningful connections with others. This is a consistent finding in study after study. By employing the simple skills outlined in these pages you will be able to increase your child's chances of enjoying a fulfilled, contented life. By helping your child understand the motions of his own heart, and training him to look into the hearts of those around him, you are nurturing skills that will increase his chances of forming loving bonds that will sustain him throughout life. As the Dalai Lama puts it: 'If you want others to be happy, practise compassion. If you want to be happy, practise compassion.' The emotional development of your child is a key to her future happiness, as well as a cornerstone of well-regulated behaviour.

 Quick summary action points

- Make conscious efforts to help your child expand his emotional vocabulary:
  —Put clear, consistent labels on your own feelings.
  —Use real-life examples, pictures and stories to identify and explain emotional reactions.

- Help your child understand that it is possible to feel different and even contradictory feelings at the same time.

- Teach children to accept their feelings – even the less-comfortable ones.

- Be clear that no one is accountable for what they *feel*, only for what they *do*.

- Help your child not to bury feelings that can lead to problems later.

- Encourage your child to become aware of the feelings and needs of others.

- Work hard to show and encourage empathy, one of the cornerstones of self-control.

- Give your child controlled exposure to positive and negative feelings, but keep the overall tone upbeat and affirming.

3
Mind control for beginners

The foundations of self-control

Whether your child is two or teenage, emotions running out of control can cause many a headache for parents – and it's not much fun for the child either. Showing your child how to manage their thoughts, feelings and actions puts them in control of a situation and gives them a real alternative to destructive behaviour.

One useful set of techniques that can be used by grown-ups as well as children comes from Cognitive Behavioural Therapy (or CBT for short). CBT has established a reputation as an effective form of 'talking therapy' for a wide range of disorders from depression to anorexia. However, at its heart lies a cluster of principles and techniques that are relevant to all of us. You certainly don't need to have psychological problems to benefit from them. In essence CBT is a way of putting the rational 'cool' mind back in control when 'hot' processing wreaks havoc with our lives. It therefore offers a very handy technology for dealing with destructive patterns of emotions and behaviour.

The really good news is that the cognitive approach is child-friendly. The principles involved are simple enough for most school-age children to grasp, and its emphasis on practical, experimental learning fits well with the way that most children operate. Unlike many therapies, CBT empowers people by equipping them with skills that they can apply in their lives. In fact, Martin Seligman, a professor at Pennsylvania, has demonstrated that if you are schooled in the basics of CBT when you are young these techniques can reduce your vulnerability to developing clinical depression.

Seligman is one of a number of influential psychologists trying to shift the discipline of psychology away from a focus on mental illness to consider instead the conditions that allow human beings to flourish and fulfil their potential. He views cognitive behavioural techniques not simply as a remedy for when things go wrong, but as an aspect of good mental hygiene that can protect people from getting sick in the first place.

This chapter will focus on how to encourage children to take greater responsibility for managing their emotions, and how to give them simple techniques to do that. When a child feels in control of his emotional life, the chances are his behaviour will reflect this – and that means fewer headaches for both child and parent alike.

Attack of the clowns – how we all see the world in different ways

Charlie, aged 4 and Tom, aged 6, are visiting the circus for the first time. Having cheered, gasped and whooped their way through seven acts, the audience is now eagerly awaiting the arrival of Big Al and his sidekick Little Mo. There is a honk of a horn and an outlandish-looking car with wobbly wheels careers into the ring. Out of it burst the clowns. Big Al promptly trips over his giant shoes, sending Little Mo head over heals into a bucket of paste. Messy mayhem ensues.

Charlie finds this hysterical and almost falls off his seat with laughter. His older brother, Tom, is also hysterical but, in his case, quite literally. The colour has drained from his face and he is screaming uncontrollably. His parents can do nothing to console him and have to take him out of the performance. Tom goes on to develop a life-long phobia of clowns (*coulrophobia* is the official term) and has not been back to the circus since.

How do we begin to explain such completely different

reactions to the same event? What ultimately determined the nature of each boy's response was not the event itself but the very different ways in which it was perceived. Whereas Charlie embraced the whole sequence as a piece of entertaining, slapstick fun, for Tom the performance tapped into something much more sinister. Each boy's emotional reaction was governed by what it meant to him.

The point is that we feel dictated to not by what happens to us but by the meanings we create around those events. No two people experience the world in exactly the same way and your child may experience things differently to you. You can't tell children what to feel, but you can steer them towards interpretations of reality that are likely to promote their happiness.

All children interpret events differently. You can't tell a child what to feel, but you can help her find constructive ways to make sense of what happens to her.

I think, I feel, I do

Our thoughts, feelings and behaviour are all connected and have a knock-on effect upon each other. It stands to reason that if we change what we think about a situation we may feel very differently about it too.

If I conclude that my friend deliberately ignored my wave as I passed by I am likely to feel hurt and affronted. However, when I recall that the friend in question is short-sighted and was not wearing glasses at the time, this information puts a new complexion on things.

The way we interpret an event determines not only our feelings but also our subsequent behaviour. A man lying in bed at night hears a noise downstairs. If he tells himself the noise was merely the cat going out of the cat flap he is likely to roll over and go back to sleep. But if he assumes there is an intruder in the house he may investigate further or call the police. Two different interpretations prompt two different behavioural responses.

> Use daily events to show how there is usually more than one way of looking at things.

This can also work in the opposite direction. In some cases simply changing behaviour can also change the way people think and feel. For example, scientists have discovered that the mere act of deliberately putting on a smile actually improves people's subjective reports of happiness.

Shaping your child's core beliefs

When we find ourselves at the mercy of negative emotions it is usually because we have managed to lose our sense of perspective – even if it doesn't feel like this at the time. Distressing feelings are usually primed by what psychologists refer to as negative automatic thoughts. These are instinctive, irrational readings of situations that tap into our vulnerabilities. They often take the form of knee-jerk reactions and can be detected in those negative comments that pop into our heads at moments of distress: 'She hates me...', 'I've messed it up again', 'I am making a fool of myself...', and so on.

While these self-critical thoughts usually relate to specific situations, they often reflect aspects of negative core beliefs. These are the more enduring, underlying convictions that sum up our feelings about ourselves and the world. The negative automatic thoughts cited above might link into generic core beliefs such as: 'I am unlovable', 'Nothing I do is ever right', 'I am worthless'.

Once entrenched, core beliefs are difficult to shift and can exert a powerful influence on the way we live. As parents it is therefore particularly important that we do our best to ensure that our children construct healthy core beliefs about themselves.

We can do this partly by the explicit messages we give them. Every time we tell our children how much we love them, when we affirm our faith in them and demonstrate our pride in their accomplishments, we are helping pro-gramme their core beliefs about themselves. Through our eyes they learn to see themselves as people who are lovable and worthwhile. When we create opportunities for our sons and daughters to use their skills and talents, or support them in accomplishing their goals, we teach them that they are capable, effective individuals who can master life's challenges and are worthy of respect.

> Make sure your children get plenty of positive feedback and create opportunities for them to excel. This will help them construct healthy core beliefs.

Conversely, if we are constantly overly critical or reproving we risk fortifying a child's secret fears: 'Nothing I do is good enough', 'I am inferior' or even 'I do not deserve to be loved'. Children are especially receptive to information given to them by the people they rely upon and, unfortu-nately, we all have a natural tendency to pay more attention to bad news than good.

Just take a moment to think about the occasions when

you are hardest on yourself. It is surprising how often at such times the inner voice of self-criticism or condemnation assumes the tones of an angry or disappointed parent. Even now you may be able to recall particular parental statements or reactions that stung you badly and may even have shaped the way you see yourself.

> Remember that the *repeated* messages you give your children will stay with them for life – make those things positive, not burdens they have to carry.

In either scenario it should be stressed that it is usually the *overall* tone and content of the messages we transmit to our children that mould core beliefs. As in all relationships we are going to say things to our children that we later regret. Please rest assured that it is unlikely that any 'one-off' statement is going to shape a child's view of herself. However, similar messages repeated day in, day out will ultimately have an impact. Even things we do not necessarily mean can shape children's self-image so, when telling your child off, make every effort to label the *behaviour* as 'bad' or 'stupid' rather than your child. The power you have as a parent gives you a great opportunity to help children develop core beliefs that will protect and fortify them throughout life. However, with that power comes the responsibility not to undermine their self-belief in moments of clumsiness, exhaustion or irritability.

Seeing only what fits

Such is the power of our core beliefs that they act like a lens that filters our perception of reality. However reasonable we may think we are, unconsciously we all have a tendency to remake the world in the image of our own convictions. We see what we are programmed to see. We may even act in ways that bring our experience into line with what we believe about ourselves – regardless of how helpful those beliefs may be for us.

We know, for example, that depressed people demonstrate certain thinking habits likely to make them feel worse. For example, a depressed child will be highly selective about what she focuses upon – usually only attending to facts that support a negative view of herself and the world. She will steadfastly ignore any information that does not fit in with those beliefs. She will be prone to 'catastrophizing' – assuming that the worst possible outcome is the most likely in any situation, even if logic suggests this is not the case. She will consistently blame herself for anything that goes wrong in her life, even events that are logically beyond her control. You will also catch her making sweeping generalizations, asserting that any negative incident is 'just typical' of the way she is.

And this isn't just about depressed children: every child has the ability to develop faulty thinking to reinforce what they believe about themselves. However careful you have been as a parent to instil positive core beliefs in your child, it's possible that he has formed some unhelpful ones of his own accord, or from things that friends or teachers have said. So if your child says things which seem odd to you, or seems unhappy or is losing control of himself, it may be that unhelpful core beliefs are creeping in. Be alert and use the techniques described below to counteract them.

> Be alert to your child showing signs of having negative beliefs about herself – in what she says or how she behaves.

Undoing bad thinking habits

So how do you unpick these sorts of bad mental habits and challenge the assumptions that underlie them? The main way is by a careful and deliberate examination of the evidence supporting the negative assumption. As in a courtroom your child needs to learn how to present the case 'for' and 'against' his thoughts and evaluate them in the light of the factual evidence. Even relatively young children can successfully learn to take to task their destructive assumptions.

When a child loses control of his behaviour you can bet that powerful feelings are working in conjunction with a cascade of negative assumptions that egg each other on until the point of meltdown is achieved. Children often over-react because they give in to catastrophic interpretations of what is happening to them. They often lose sight of the bigger picture, get swallowed up in the intensity of their own distress and disconnect their immediate experience from wider webs of meaning that could otherwise have provided an emotional safety net. Furthermore, children often take their own destabilized emotions as further evidence of the truth of their upsetting thoughts.

Picture a nervous toddler who has wandered off in a department store and has lost sight of his mother. Although he could probably not articulate his thoughts explicitly the mental process he experiences would probably look something like this:

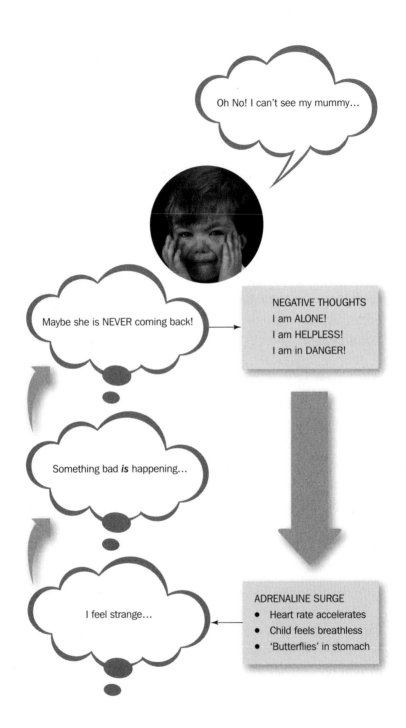

It is easy to see how this catastrophic cycle of thought and feeling can escalate. Before long this child has been reduced to a state of extreme distress. Of course, when his mother does find him again he has a new experience that hopefully will weaken the assumption that briefly losing contact with his parent means he has been abandoned.

Teaching your child to challenge negative thinking and keep a cool head is not something that can be achieved overnight. However, the ability to neutralize upsetting thoughts is very useful for a child and can become the foundation of a robust self-image. It will also help put your child back in the driving seat of his emotions. That, at least is the theory. In the next few sections we will think about how you can apply the cognitive approach in practice and, more importantly, teach your child to do the same.

Joining the dots

To a child the fact that her thoughts affect her feelings and vice versa is not necessarily obvious. Yet this is a connection to which children need to be introduced as early as possible if the impact of negative thinking is to be limited.

> Take every opportunity to show your child how changing the way you think can change the way you feel.

With a school-age child you can introduce this concept in a number of low-key ways. Making explicit connections between what people think and what they feel is something that can be done in a number of everyday situations. It is largely a question of picking up on opportunities in everyday conversation with your child. Say, for example, your son reports that he saw another child crying in the playground during break. Typically, these kinds of conversations will run as follows:

> **Child**: I saw Matthew crying in the playground at break today . . .
>
> **Mother**: Did you darling? What made him upset?
>
> **Child**: I don't know. I think it was because Gary and Roger didn't play football with him like they normally do.
>
> **Mother**: That's a shame. Maybe you could ask him to play with you?

Although the mother helpfully offers a solution, demonstrating some basic problem-solving skills, she misses the opportunity to challenge her son's assumption that events (rather than their interpretation) produce emotions. The same conversation could have been handled as follows:

> **Child**: Matthew was crying in the playground at break today . . .
>
> **Mother**: Was he darling? Why *do you think* he was so unhappy?
>
> **Child**: I dunno. Probably because Gary and Roger didn't play football with him like they normally do.
>
> **Mother**: Oh dear! So *what did Matthew make of that*?
>
> **Child**: Well, probably that they didn't like him any more.
>
> **Mother**: Hmm, well if that was what *he was thinking* I can see why he might have felt sad. But aren't the three of them friends? Was there some other reason why they didn't play with him today?

Child: Maybe because he was late out after the lesson and they thought he was swapping football cards with Mike like he did yesterday.

Mother: Did anyone point that out to him? How do you think Matthew would have felt *if he had realized* that was the reason?

Child: I guess he probably wouldn't have been so upset. What's for tea?

Prompting children to make connections between what other people think and feel in everyday situations lays a valuable foundation for handling their own difficult feelings.

> Gently challenge your child's assumptions about other people's feelings. 'Why do you think he felt that?', 'Could there have been another reason he was sad?', etc.

Using TV and books

Stories that involve elements of disguise or deception are particularly handy for making this association. They underline discrepancies between what a 'misled' character believes and the reality of their situation.

In the children's cartoon *Scooby-Doo* a team of not-so-fearless detectives are regularly called upon to investigate sightings of a ghost or monster. The format of each episode dictates that the appearance of the ghost provokes much histrionic behaviour – especially from the hapless Shaggy and Scooby who will spend much of the episode racing down corridors with the 'ghost' in hot pursuit. At the denouement of each episode the supernatural fiend is unveiled, usually turning out to be Mrs Delaney, the vengeful aunt, or Hector, the embittered gardener. The cast breathes a collective sigh of relief and the credits roll.

As usual, their unfounded fear was based upon a mis-perception. This is a point that can be made to even young children: 'What did Shaggy feel when he *thought* it was a ghost ...?', 'What did he feel when he *realized* it was just a man with a sheet on his head ...?' Simple questions like these introduce children to the notion that what people feel and do is strongly influenced by what they believe.

Using drawings

You can also introduce the relationship between thoughts and feelings using drawings of stick figures with blank faces and thought bubbles. Give your child a scenario and ask her to come up with a corresponding thought. Then invite her to draw the expression that goes with what the figure is thinking. For example, Joanna, the stick figure in a picture, may have just been told she is going to the zoo that afternoon. Most children will put a positive cognition in the thought bubble: 'I'm a lucky girl', 'The trip will be fun', 'Today is a happy day', etc. When asked how that thought makes Joanna feel they will obligingly draw a smile on her face.

The next stage is to demonstrate what happens to Joanna's feelings when events take a turn for the worse. Perhaps when they arrive the zoo is closed or while walking round she drops her ice cream. The process is repeated, usually eliciting a negative thought ('Everything's spoilt ...') and a sad face. At each stage the adult makes the link between what Joanna is thinking and the emotions she is experiencing.

The final phase is to present the child with another stick figure on which the adult draws a neutral or more cheerful expression. The child is asked: 'Can you think of *anything* that we can put in this thought bubble that might make Joanna's face change from *this* [indicates 'sad' Joanna] to *this* [pointing to image of a more cheerful/neutral Joanna]?'

With a little encouragement, most children will volunteer a more upbeat thought involving a shift in perspective or even a solution to the problem. Examples might include: 'We can always come back tomorrow when the zoo is open' or 'My daddy will buy me another ice cream so it doesn't matter'. The quality of the content is not that important. What is vital is that the child begins to understand that what goes on in her head directly influences what she feels.

When using this technique at home you will have the advantage of being able to use an example direct from your son or daughter's own experience, maybe at the very time this is most relevant. Using drawing makes it a relaxed and familiar way of raising the subject.

Use stick figures and thought bubbles to show the connection between thoughts and feelings, and how thinking something positive can make you feel happier.

Trapping negative thoughts

Spotting our habitual negative thoughts can prove tricky for adults and children alike but it is an essential skill to master. Many of these thoughts have been so well-rehearsed in our heads that we are barely conscious of them as thoughts at all. Like the wallpaper that we no longer notice when we enter a room, our negative thoughts can assume a taken-for-granted quality that can render them all but invisible. They also flit through consciousness so quickly that it can be hard to isolate them.

In the case of children, cognitive immaturity means that their subjective readings of reality can all too easily take on the status of undisputed fact: 'No one likes me... that's just the way it is.' Seeing himself in this way, Alec screens out the time when Richard and Mike invited him to join them on the cinema trip. Carrying this belief with him, when Alec does find himself in social situations he doesn't think he's welcome. He expects rejection, and copes either by holding back or by alienating other children before they can reject him. Thinking and behaving in this way make it harder for Alec to make friends and see himself in a different light. The problem is now perpetuating itself.

A child in Alec's situation will need support to understand and break the cycle in which he has become trapped, and some of the techniques we will be looking at will hopefully show how that can best be achieved. However, Alec also needs to be encouraged to shift the focus away from himself. Learning to show an interest in other people and appreciate what he has to offer in social situations will equip Alec to collect fresh evidence that he can then use to challenge his negative assumptions about himself. There are some more tips about how to handle relationships with other children in Chapter 6.

Know your enemy

In order to help younger children identify negative thoughts it can be useful to give their source a concrete, visual representation. In western culture we are all familiar with the image of the devil and the angel at our shoulder, each trying to grab our attention. What your child needs to know is that we all have a 'saboteur' or part of ourselves that is hell-bent on making our lives miserable. This invisible enemy is the source of negativity, pessimism, destructive criticism, and all of those thoughts that make it hard for us to feel very good about ourselves.

From the age of 5 I often ask children to invent a character who will give their saboteur some sort of tangible form. Younger children struggle with abstract concepts but most will happily engage with the task of drawing a picture or making a model of their saboteur.

You can introduce the idea as follows:

'Most of us have a voice in our head that can say really mean things to us and make us feel sad and worried. Can you give me an example of some of the sorts of things that voice might say to you [prompt with your own example if the child is finding it hard]. I want you to imagine the sort of person or creature who might be saying those sorts of things to you. Let's pretend that this voice in your head also has a body. What sort of creature or thing do you think it might be? It's your creature so you can make it anything you want.'

Some children create monsters or witches; others come up with thunder clouds or animals. By all means respond to the emotional qualities of what your child depicts ('Gosh those claws look sharp!', 'The fact you can't see her face makes her look quite spooky...') but be careful not to impose your own assumptions or start adding your own ideas. Instead follow your curiosity and use open questions to encourage your child to flesh out her creation. Younger children will need these questions to be quite concrete:

- Where does he/she/it live?

- What sort of things does your monster like doing?

- How do its weapons work?

It goes without saying that this approach will need to be modified for older children, although the concept of a personal saboteur is still one that many teenagers (and adults for that matter) find appealing. For teenagers and older children who may find this all a bit babyish, useful analogies can be drawn with computers. For example, negative automatic thoughts can be compared to computer viruses capable of corrupting system software and causing malfunctions.

> When a child is struggling with negative thoughts, get him to
> draw or model the 'baddie' – the character who whispers
> negative things to him. Then show him how to defeat the
> baddie by choosing to ignore its tactics.

It is worth noting that although most people experience negative thoughts in the form of subliminal 'voices' in their heads, some individuals also experience these thoughts in a more visual form, perhaps picturing themselves failing or 'seeing' their worst-case scenario playing out in front of their mind's eye.

Once your child has established what form her saboteur will take the next step is to give it a name. After that you need to think with your child about its armoury and the tactics that it uses to make her feel bad. The easiest way to do this is to think about the kind of things the saboteur typically says when it wants to make her feel sad, worthless or anxious. What your child comes up with in response to this can often provide you with important insights into the nature of your child's fears. The Ugly Monster might tell John that he is a 'pathetic weakling' or the Dinosaur of Doom might growl at Jenny that 'No one will ever want to be her friend'.

Once you have collected an adequate sample of critical self-statements you can examine them together and see whether you can discover any clues as to the way the saboteur operates. With a little luck you will be able to establish several important principles: what the saboteur tells you is almost always a distortion of the truth. Your saboteur is a liar. And it doesn't play fair. However, you also need to let your child know that she is powerful enough to defeat it.

At this stage the important thing is that your child is learning to articulate and group together self-statements that share a common quality. By learning to recognize the distinctive 'voice' of their personal saboteur children can start to differentiate between thoughts that are helpful and those that are less so. A category of 'bad' thoughts is created that your son or daughter knows must be approached with caution.

As your child learns to equate negative thoughts with the activity of his saboteur, he is already beginning to 'bracket' such thoughts and no longer accept them at face value. He is learning to catch out self-defeating tendencies in himself and familiarize himself with the ways they undermine his self-esteem.

Personifying your child's negativity in this way gives you both an accessible, common language to talk about fears and destructive thought patterns. Being able to think with your son about where a specific thought comes from ('Is Terrorix trying to slip in another thought bomb to make you feel bad, James?') is a helpful way of getting a child into the right mindset. Framed in this way, your child will also readily understand why the enemy's schemes must be met with active resistance.

The monster disposal squad

A further advantage for children who are too young to challenge the saboteur's statements using an analytical or rational strategy is that by giving their negativity a tangible form they can use simple visualization techniques to help counter its effects. A boy whose saboteur took the form of a fire-breathing dragon imagined himself with a magic suit of armour that reflected the blast back towards its source whenever it tried to make him feel afraid. A 6-year-old girl I knew equipped herself with a large vacuum cleaner to suck up her 'angry blue cloud'. Shrinking the saboteur down until it can be popped in a matchbox is popular, and children often invent imaginative (and often quite violent!) technologies to silence the voice of their inner critic.

While this is not the same as being able to unpick negative thoughts in the way they can when they get older, being able to picture themselves taking charge of the situation gives many children a sense of control over thoughts and feelings that can otherwise overpower them.

What's the damage?

Once a negative thought has successfully been identified the next stage is to look at its emotional impact. If you have used the techniques above to sensitize your child to different feelings, detecting and labelling the resulting emotions should not be too difficult. However, when attempting to apply cognitive strategies to manage feelings it is also very helpful to try and rate their intensity. The reason is that it provides a good test of any antidote thoughts your child generates later. Does the antidote thought effectively reduce the force of the original emotions? Unless those have been rated it will be hard to tell.

To show how this works, we will use the example of Tabitha who is 9 years old. It is tea time and, uncharacteristically, Tabitha has been in a foul mood since she returned home from school. She has been tormenting her little sister mercilessly and fighting with her brother over who gets to control what they watch on TV. Her mother doesn't know what has got into her and is swiftly approaching the limits of her patience.

However, rather than shouting at her, she takes Tabitha aside, gives her some frank feedback about her behaviour and asks whether she can think of any reason why she is finding it so hard to behave herself? Tabitha reminds her mother that tomorrow is the day of her Grade Three piano exam. Although she has been working conscientiously towards this for months it transpires that Tabitha is suffering from a last-minute crisis of confidence.

> Ask a badly behaved child if they can think of any reason they are finding it hard to behave like normal today. If the answer turns out to be a worry, explore the negative thoughts behind it.

Working together, Tabitha and her mother brainstorm several negative thoughts that might be fuelling Tabitha's anxiety and bad behaviour:

I'm going to make a mistake...

I'm just no good at piano...

If I don't pass I'll be a failure...

Out of these three it is the last that appears to be the most relevant because it is producing the strongest emotional reaction. This is Tabitha's 'hot thought' and her rating of the emotions it generates in her is shown at the top of the facing page:

'If I don't pass I'll be a failure'	
Afraid	4/10
Miserable	7/10
Helpless	8/10
Angry	5/10

The very process of gauging the strength of feelings is an important stage in engaging the more objective 'cooling' centres of the brain. Emotions are being experienced but also considered and quantified. Younger children will obviously require a simplified scale (a little/quite a bit/a lot) and teenagers can usually handle percentages. However, the principle is the same.

> Teach your child to rate the intensity of his feelings: 'If 1 is not angry at all and 10 is the angriest you can imagine, how angry are you?'

Looking at the breakdown of Tabitha's feelings it becomes easier to understand why she had been throwing her weight around with her siblings. Asserting her dominance was one way of compensating for her underlying feelings of vulnerability.

Sometimes your child may not be aware of the buried 'hot thought' that is driving his emotions or the negative thoughts identified may feel a bit tenuous. You can use the 'downward arrow' technique to bring your child closer to the thought that is really driving his anxiety. This simply involves probing each of the thoughts or aspects of the situation and exploring their implications using simple questions such as:

- What would be the worst thing about that?
- What does that mean for you if that is true?
- Why would that be so terrible?

This process is repeated with each answer to peel back the layers and get closer to the core anxiety. In the example below Harry's negative automatic thoughts are in bold type:

Harry: I don't want to go to school today.

Parent: Why's that? What's so bad about today?

Harry: We've got that geography test.

Parent: Why is that such bad news then?

Harry: Well **I'm bound to screw up again**.

Parent: And if you did? What would happen?

Harry: Umm... well **everyone would laugh at me**.

Parent: Okay. That doesn't sound great, but what would be the hardest part of that for you if it did happen?

Harry: It means **I'm dumb**.

Parent: Well I certainly don't agree with you on that one – but let's pretend it's true for a moment: why does being clever matter so much?

Harry: Well, who wants to be friends with a thicko?

[If I am stupid no one will like me]

Parent: But do you feel that no one likes you at school?

Harry: Sometimes.

Parent: What would that mean about you if it was true?

Harry: Maybe that **I'm just no good**.

You can see how by using the downward arrow technique it was possible to get closer to the real 'hot thought' that was making Harry reluctant to go to school. The anxieties about his academic performance were a bit of a red herring. Harry's underlying problem was his perception that he was unpopular and his distorted belief that people with few friends must, by definition, have something wrong with them.

Weighing the evidence

The next stage is to help your child evaluate the truth status of the negative thought. As in a court of law, this is done by carefully weighing the evidence which supports the negative thought against other information that might discredit it. Explain to your child how the legal system works, and tell him that he will need to play the role of both prosecution and defence barrister in order to establish if a 'thought crime' is being committed.

Firstly, invite your child to think about the various factors that make the negative belief seem true. Has he had similar experiences that reinforce that belief? Are the factors emotional or are there any logical or common sense grounds that support it? At this stage resist the temptation to start analysing whatever your child says. Let the reasons all come out. It is important to have a genuinely open mind: if there are grounds to take the belief seriously then these need to be given due weight. This approach only works if you are both honest. Try and brainstorm as comprehensive a list as possible.

Having gathered the evidence in support of the belief,

your child then needs to draw up a second column. This time he is cast in the role of prosecutor. This second list should include anything that contradicts or challenges the authority of the negative belief. Are there any rational grounds on which to object to the belief? Has your child had *any* experiences that appear to contradict it? If so it cannot be completely true. Are there reasons to suggest that the belief is too extreme or represents a biased view of reality?

> Work with your child to find examples or evidence that *support* the negative belief – and then ask them to think of evidence or examples that suggest it's *not* true.

It will be very helpful if your child becomes familiar with the common thinking errors in the box above. Our negative beliefs often reflect these kinds of distortions and familiarity with them naturally makes them much easier to spot.

If your child is finding it hard to pick the negative thought apart, a useful strategy can be to ask him to think about what a friend might say about the belief or whether the belief would be endorsed by someone (real or fictional) that your child admires: 'Do you think that Uncle Dave would see it that way, Luke? What would *he* have to say about it?

Some common thinking traps to watch out for ...

● **Catastrophizing** – assuming the worst and seeing the consequences as more terrible than they need to be ('I've made a complete fool of myself. I won't *ever* be able to show my face in there again...').

- **Mind-reading** – ascribing motives, intentions and judgements to other people without any real evidence ('They're bound to all hate me now...', 'He obviously tripped me up on purpose').

- **Overgeneralizing** – making sweeping statements and assumptions on the basis of a one-off incident ('I've missed the bus ... Why does everything *always* go wrong for me?').

- **Selective perception** – only looking at the facts that support your prejudiced view ('He wasn't smiling so I've obviously upset him').

- **Using emotive language** – putting things in exaggerated or graphic terms that make things seem worse than they are ('I'm such an *idiot*. No wonder people *can't stand* me').

- **Unrealistic expectations** – making distorted assumptions about what should happen in a situation, often leading the person to take excessive responsibility or set unrealistic standards of behaviour for themselves or others ('I *should* have seen it coming...', 'He *ought* to have done much better than that...', 'I *mustn't* fail again...').

- **Personalizing** – taking things personally, even when events are just down to chance or bad luck ('And now my dog needs an operation. Someone up there has really got it in for me').

- **Black and white thinking** – seeing things in polarized 'all or nothing terms' ('If they don't agree with me, they must be my enemy', 'If I don't come first I'll be a failure').

In her capacity as prosecutor, your offspring is also entitled to cross-examine the defence witnesses. This means that she needs to look carefully at the statements in the first column and see whether she can spot any flaws in the argument, and inconsistencies or logical weaknesses. These are added to the case against the negative thought. In Tabitha's example her final list of evidence 'for' and 'against' looked like this:

Belief in the dock: 'If I don't pass I'll be a failure.'

Evidence for ... (Things telling me my belief is true)	Evidence against ... (Things telling me my belief is untrue)
My strong gut feeling that my belief is true.	My feelings cannot always be trusted. (Remember how you fancied Robin Wainwright in Year 2!)
Ellie Jones is really successful and she has passed her grade 8 violin already.	Even successful people make mistakes and get things wrong sometimes.
Mrs Roddick says that anyone can do *anything* if they try hard enough. I have tried really hard so if I still fail that must mean I'm not as good as most people.	Making mistakes is part and parcel of learning something. All success involves some failure along the way. Mrs Roddick was just trying to make us all believe in ourselves.
I certainly *felt* like a failure last time when I mucked up my cycling proficiency and nearly everyone else in the class did really well.	But even though I didn't do that well compared with the others I still passed. In fact there were two other people who didn't do as well as I did – I think Sue actually failed the test.

I knew I was going to do badly in the race at sports day and that turned out just how I thought it would.	Even if I fail my grade 3 tomorrow it will not be the end of the world. My family will still love me, I still have my friends and lots of things I am good at and enjoy. Perhaps I need a different definition of success?
Lots of people are better than me at piano.	It is crazy to see myself as a 'success' or a 'failure' based on just this one thing.
Everyone will be really disappointed in me if I do fail.	I can only do my best. If I need to I can always take it again. I will probably be the most disappointed and I don't need to make myself responsible for other people's feelings. Anyway, the people I love have never minded that much when I have stuffed up in the past.
Grandad always says you are either a winner or a loser in life. Winners don't mess things up.	I have practised hard and my music teacher says I am ready. It is probably only my fear telling me I won't pass. The chances are I will. In the worst case scenario I can take it again.

Any other offers?

Having reviewed all the evidence for and against, your child needs to see whether he can come up with an alternative thought that more accurately reflects the newly perceived truth of the situation. This needs to be a *realistic* thought based on the working through of all the various arguments. Simply replacing the negative belief with idealized, wishful thinking will not have any impact upon your child's emotions. It has to ring true.

The more adaptive thought may be taken straight from one or more of the elements in that second column, or it may simply be a modification of the original thought that acknowledges some elements of 'second column' thinking. Some of the reasons given in the second column may be much more pertinent than others.

Tabitha's eventual antidote thought was as follows:

> *'Failing one exam would not make me a failure as a person, however badly I want to pass. None of the most important things in my life will change if I do fail. I don't have to be perfect at everything to be a good person.'*

At the end of this process Tabitha rated her new belief as having a strength of 8 out of 10. The effectiveness of this new thought was then tested out by rerating her original feelings as honestly as possible.

Feelings	Strength
Afraid	2/10
Miserable	1/10
Helpless	2/10
Angry	2/10

Review all the points for and against the belief being true and see if, between you, it's possible to find a new belief; one that is based on the evidence. This is the antidote thought.

Troubleshooting

As can be seen, for Tabitha her new 'antidote' thought produced a marked reduction in the strength of her unpleasant feelings. However, if you find that your child's emotion ratings are not shifting significantly check out the following:

- Did you identify the relevant hot thought(s) in the first place?

- Has your child really grappled with the evidence for and against – or is he giving himself (or you) pat answers based on what he ought to think or what you want to hear?

- Are there more powerful underlying beliefs or core assumptions that are fuelling the problem and need to be addressed directly?

- Does the new alternative thought reflect the truth of the situation rather than a sanitized version of it?

Over to you

Although the principles of the cognitive approach are quite straightforward, the consistent application of the techniques to real-life situations predictably proves more challenging for some children. The cognitive behavioural approach is more than a ragbag of techniques: it is also a mental discipline. To establish it as a consistent part of your child's orientation to life will require coaching and support.

To begin with, the whole processes of identifying and appraising automatic thoughts can seem a rather long-winded business. However, please do not be tempted to miss out stages because you weaken the usefulness of the technique if it is approached in a slapdash manner. Like many other skills that are painful to acquire in their early stages, these strategies will come to feel much more natural and spontaneous in time. Eventually your child will be able to perform these stages in her head.

When a child comes to see a professional for therapy, the time available is usually quite limited. Within the scope of just a few weeks the child must be introduced to the cognitive behavioural model, taught the necessary techniques and given tasks and homework relevant to the target problem.

As a parent, however, you are in an enviable position. You not only have time on your side, but a privileged insight into the struggles your child faces on a daily basis. You will have countless opportunities to help your child make sense of these situations and his reactions to them. You can be there 'in the field' to gently prompt and remind, to reinforce your child's efforts and gently pick him up when he is struggling to apply the techniques. All of this is hard work. But, if you stick with it you will see results.

> Take every opportunity to pick out negative thoughts and examine them – in time it gets much quicker and easier and eventually your child will do it automatically without you prompting.

Once they get good at this process you will see the benefits start to manifest themselves in your children's behaviour. Most children who learn these techniques become less prone to panic in the face of distressing feelings and less inclined to 'act out' as a way of coping with them. They stop taking their fears and upset at face value because they have a reliable strategy for dealing with their emotions. Being less at the mercy of their feelings puts young people into a position in which they have more choice about how they will respond to them. And that's important.

 ## Quick summary action points

- What we feel about any event, and how we react to it, depends upon our interpretation. Don't assume your child sees things as you do – or as her siblings do.

- Use everyday situations to teach your child the connections between thoughts, feelings and behaviour. Ask questions like 'why do you think . . .' and 'how did that make you/him feel?'

- Watch out for negative and biased thinking in your child's way of looking at herself and the world.

- Help your child recognize that upsetting thoughts usually involve a distortion of reality.

- Encourage your child to give a concrete form to his inner saboteur. Personifying the source of your child's negative thoughts can make the task of doing battle with them less daunting.

- Practise cognitive strategies with your child to analyse and manage distressing feelings:
  —Teach him how to identify destructive 'hot thoughts'.
  —Show her how to review the evidence both 'for' and 'against'.
  —Enable your child to become skilled at generating more balanced 'alternative thoughts'.

4

Becoming indestructible

Nurturing resilience in young people

For most parents the idea of a child being depressed or anxious is hard to imagine. We either think it won't happen to our children, or possibly even dismiss the idea that such well-cared-for children could be depressed. What we can't ignore is that numerous painstaking studies have clearly shown that depression is not only endemic but also that it is striking earlier and earlier.

Although the facts are alarming, some children are more vulnerable to depression than others. However, as parents we can't afford to bury our heads in the sand and pretend that this could never happen to our own son or daughter.

Good parenting means being aware that it happens, being ready to deal with it if it does and, most of all, actively putting in place strategies to prevent it. After all, if you have it in your power to give your child the best possible chance of a healthy mind as well as a healthy body, why wouldn't you?

We all need to pay attention to the childhood depression figures, because the reality is that depressed and anxious states of mind can often be the root cause of 'bad behaviour'. Parents need to be mindful of this possibility both when confronting such behaviour and putting in place strategies to deal with it.

Fortunately, there is much we can do to instil mental habits that can protect children against developing conditions like depression and anxiety. In this chapter we will look at some of the key principles behind these good habits, and show you how you can encourage your child to cultivate them.

Spotting the problem

GPs sometimes refer to depression as the common cold of psychiatry, but this analogy hardly does justice to the incapacitating impact that clinical depression and anxiety can have on people's lives. Sufferers from depression don't only feel down and find it hard to motivate themselves. The condition may also affect concentration, memory, sleeping and eating patterns. Depressed people can become withdrawn, irritable and feel hopeless or full of self-loathing.

In children, depression is often missed because it doesn't always resemble its adult counterpart. Because of the way children handle emotional turbulence, rather than becoming classically flat and withdrawn a depressed child may become more aggressive, rude or generally difficult to manage. The first you may know about it are reports of misbehaviour or poor performance at school.

Alternatively, depressed children may respond by regressing or translate their emotional distress into physical symptoms – stomach complaints, headaches, and other aches and pains. Disturbed nights or recurrent nightmares may be another warning sign that something is awry. As a parent it is worth familiarizing yourself with the symptoms in the checklist below.

Depression checklist

✔ Lasting low, sad mood that does not shift

✔ Child seems unusually tetchy, irritable or angry

✔ Child complains of feeling worthless: 'I am bad', 'I am stupid', 'No one likes me'.

- ✔ Child seems flat: loses interest in preferred activities
- ✔ Starts sleeping more or has disturbed nights
- ✔ Puts on weight or loses it
- ✔ Finds it hard to concentrate and remember things
- ✔ Becomes either sluggish or constantly 'on the go'
- ✔ Reports thoughts or dreams of dying or suicide.

Just because your child is behaving badly does not, of course, necessarily mean she is depressed or stressed. However, if such behaviour is unusual, it is always worth considering whether this might be the case.

Where do we draw the line?

Even if it were possible to guarantee your child would never suffer from a diagnosable depression or anxiety disorder the information in this chapter is still relevant to you. In the west our disease approach to mental health encourages us to 'bracket off' such states as identifiable illnesses. We have a whole system of diagnostic criteria to draw a clear line in the sand between 'normal' experience and an official mental illness. For example, to qualify for a formal diagnosis of clinical depression you have to feel down most of the day or stop enjoying things consistently for at least a two-week period, as well as presenting a selection of other symptoms.

However, while they serve a purpose, these diagnostic cut-offs also disguise the fact that conditions like depression and anxiety are also spectrum disorders. We all feel down at times. Sometimes we find ourselves in a blue funk that may even last for days. We all get anxious and jittery or have periods during which we know we are approaching the end of our tether and even notice ourselves worrying obsessively about certain things.

Normally these episodes pass. We bounce back and our symptoms have been neither severe nor sufficiently enduring to earn a formal diagnosis. However, while our experiences during those times may be less intense and extreme than that of a card-carrying depressive, there is probably more overlap than we would like to believe. Most of us are quite good at deleting the bad times, especially if our reactions during them feel uncharacteristic, but the truth is that even the least depressed and anxious of us have periods when we feel like depressed or anxious people and, more importantly, start thinking like them.

> All children can have times of feeling depressed or anxious – even if that isn't a permanent state.

Children, in particular, are capable of shifting into different moods and states of mind very rapidly. Like all of us, they can inhabit depressed or anxious states without ever reaching the threshold for diagnosis. While they occur these 'micro-episodes' can still have a knock-on effect upon your child's behaviour. Unless they learn to tackle the associated thought patterns, there is a risk that these bad habits become engrained, making a child potentially vulnerable to depressive illness later in life.

Feeling blue, thinking blue

In the previous chapter we introduced a cognitive behavioural model that stresses the way in which thoughts, feelings, behaviour and physical sensations are all connected and influence each other. What researchers have discovered is that depressed people, and those vulnerable to depression, both demonstrate a characteristic style of thinking. It will come as no surprise to discover that if you consistently think like a depressed person the chances are you will become depressed. The same is true for sufferers from chronic anxiety.

Martin Seligman has highlighted that there are distinctive differences in the way that depressed and non-depressed people explain the things that happen to them. The following is an example that will hopefully illustrate these crucial differences, so that you can become more aware of patterns to challenge in your own child's thinking, and beneficial habits that it can be useful to encourage.

Aaron is 12 years old. He has recently joined a local swimming club and there is a gala at the weekend. He is desperately keen to be selected, but when the coach announces the team at the next practice Aaron's name is not on the list. He feels crushed and sick with disappointment. Seeing how upset he is his father asks him what is wrong. Aaron shouts at his dad that he 'doesn't want to talk about it' and storms off to his room. When he has calmed down sufficiently he finally offers the following explanation:

> **Aaron:** I don't know why I even joined the stupid swimming club. I will never be any good. There are loads of people who are better than me. I should have got the message after last Thursday: my times are too slow. Mr Jackson obviously thinks I am a complete loser. Maybe I just don't have any talent after all. I wanted to do this so badly. Why does nothing ever work out for me, Dad? It's just not fair . . .

> **Father:** Hold on a minute ... Didn't you tell me that you came third in the breaststroke heats on Thursday?
>
> **Aaron:** Yeah, but that was just a fluke and I wasn't able to keep it up in the other races. Dennis said there had been some bug going round so I probably only did alright because the others weren't fully better. Anyway I didn't get picked: I'm just rubbish. I'd better just get used to it.

When we look closer at Aaron's comments we can find all the hallmarks of a classically depressive style of thinking. Look at the way Aaron positions himself with regards to this disappointing turn of events. Firstly, he doesn't see his failure to be selected as a temporary setback but as a permanent obstacle to his *ever* being in the team. He concludes that he 'will *never* be any good' and blames factors such as an innate lack of talent that are enduring and unchangeable.

This is typical of the way depressed people think. When bad things happen they tend to see them as indicative of a *permanent* state whereas non-depressive people are much more inclined to see the problem as a temporary one. More optimistic people are psychologically more open to reversals of their bad fortune in future, whereas depressives are disposed to think that only good situations will not last.

> Be aware of depressed thinking signs – that all things are bad and will stay bad, that nothing ever works or is any good, and that this is always happening to me.

Secondly, Aaron explains his failure to make the team in *global* terms rather than factors specific to a particular context. A non-depressed thinking style might have pro-

duced explanations that highlight exceptional circumstances: perhaps the coach felt that as a new member of the
club to be put in the team at such an early stage might have
put Aaron under too much pressure? Maybe the team for
that particular gala had been selected before Aaron joined?

Aaron, however, automatically regards his plight as a
reflection of a universal principle that '*nothing* ever works
out for him'. His failure to make the team is taken as
further evidence of what an unfair place the world in
general is proving to be. He has not just failed to make the
team for one race meeting: in his head he is now a 'loser',
a position that has much wider ramifications. From his
despondent vantage point Aaron can see nothing but
further disappointment ahead in all walks of life.

Thirdly, when bad things happen to depressive people
they tend to blame *internal* qualities in themselves rather
than external aspects of the situation. In Aaron's mind the
outcome of the selection process is due to the 'fact' that he
is 'rubbish' and evidently viewed as such by the coach. As
far as he is concerned, he has not been selected because he
is inferior to the other swimmers. His lack of talent (a
fixed, person-centred explanation) means that he might as
well give up.

Aaron doesn't ask himself whether the explanation for
the bad event might have nothing to do with him or be due
to factors beyond his control as a non-depressive thinker
would. He doesn't stop to consider that the coach might
not have noticed his outstanding performance in the
breaststroke trials, or that there might be factors shaping
the selection process of which he is unaware. For Aaron
this is a personal failure for which he must take sole
responsibility.

Interestingly, when his father attempts to offer him some consolation by reminding him of his breaststroke perform-ance Aaron reverses his strategy. This *good* event is not seen as due to any skill or ability on his part: it was 'a fluke'. Unlike his failure, Aaron's success is seen as tem-porary and, as an exception to the rule, has no broader implications of any value. Other people's performance must have been influenced by illness. Aaron brushes aside evidence that does not fit with his bleak vision of himself and the world.

A different perspective . . .

Sally joined the swimming club the same time as Aaron. Like him, she also was not picked to be in the team. And like Aaron she also felt initially disappointed. However, the sense that she makes of the situation is very different. Witness the conversation that she has with her mother the same evening.

Mother: Are you okay Sally? You are pretty quiet this evening . . .

Sally: I am just really hacked off. I didn't get picked for the swim team on Saturday.

Mother: Oh, I am sorry to hear that.

Sally: Well, I suppose it doesn't matter too much. There are lots of other competitions coming up this season . . . If I train hard I am sure I can still make the team. Maybe Mr Jackson didn't want to take a risk with me this time round? It is quite an important match for the club. He didn't pick that new boy

Aaron either and he got a really fast time in the breaststroke trials on Thursday. Maybe he wants to play it safe for the time being.

Mother: But you are really good at swimming. I don't understand.

Sally: I suppose I just have to prove that to Mr Jackson. Last Thursday I did have a bit of an off day and my back was still quite sore after gym on Wednesday so I wasn't at my best last week. Maybe I should let him see that medal I won at school. I just need to show him what I can do. There's plenty of time before the end of the season.

Sally's outlook is obviously much more upbeat, but closer analysis also reveals a very different attributional style. Firstly, unlike Aaron, she does not blame herself but looks around for exceptional *situational* factors that might explain the coach's decision. Secondly, she sees the decision as a *temporary* setback that she can reverse by training harder and drawing herself to Mr Jackson's attention. She doesn't dismiss her failure to qualify as indicative of a lack of talent but the result of 'having an off-day'. Moreover, unlike Aaron, Sally does not believe her current exclusion from the team has any broader implications for her performance, either as a swimmer or in any other area of her life. Thirdly, she keeps the significance of her failure tightly contained and *localized*.

It is not difficult to appreciate how, when repeated and ingrained over time, such contrasting explanatory styles can have a profound impact on a child's mood and mental robustness. Children who habitually think like Sally have been proven to have a much greater resilience to depression, whereas the Aarons of this world are likely to merge into the 10 per cent of people who experience clinical depression at some point in their lives. So as a concerned parent how can you help?

Supporting healthy thinking

You can help your child develop the attitudes of a non-depressive stance by making both of you conscious of the way your child is interpreting what is happening to her. If your child is not too down in the dumps you can use the three dimensions we have just outlined to ask pertinent questions that will encourage her to view things differently. You can also challenge the key dimensions of unduly pessimistic styles of thinking directly.

Response	Functions
'Aaron, I understand how disappointed you feel at the moment but you are talking as if not qualifying for this one gala means that you will never be on the team. What makes you think that?'	• Acknowledges the emotional reality of the situation • Challenges perceived *permanence* of the bad event • Invites a more objective review of available evidence
'I am totally confident that if you train hard you will make faster and faster times. But even if you never get picked that doesn't make you a "loser" or a "rubbish" person. Do you choose your friends on the basis of what they can do? Maybe you and I need to do some thinking about what makes someone valuable ...'	• Challenges *generalized significance* of bad event • Disputes underlying core assumption: 'I am worthless' • Introduces a new frame of reference and gives an invitation to think more flexibly

'You are being really hard on yourself, Aaron. Maybe the reason has nothing to do with you. Let's see whether we can think of any other reasons why Mr Jackson might not have picked you on this occasion . . .'	• Challenges *self-focused* explanation of bad event • Explores other alternatives • Invites rational appraisal to counter emotional, knee-jerk reaction

> Help your child think positively and optimistically, with a balanced outlook. Teach constructive responses to bad events.

As always, try and lead by example. Children do absorb and often imitate the way the adults around them react. The years we spend as parents can be a hard, demanding period of our lives when our responsibilities can weigh heavily upon us and we enjoy less personal freedom. However rewarding we find our role as parents, most of us struggle at times. Under pressure it's all too easy to take things personally, lose perspective and feel that life has got it in for us. Nevertheless, our influence means that we need to keep an eye on our reactions and interpretations. Relatively subtle differences in approach can set powerful precedents for children that can shape their thinking styles for years to come.

> Check how *you* are interpreting events – make sure you aren't teaching your children bad habits by accident. If you realize you've made a mistake, point it out and say why.

Try and foster a family culture in which everyone, regardless of age, is invited to share responsibility for promoting the well-being of other family members. Once they are old enough to understand these principles, give your children permission to challenge you when they spot an unhelpful attitude or negative way of thinking.

When you get it wrong (as we all do at times) don't hesitate to point out your own mistakes. For some children it is far easier to learn from your errors than from their own. You are also making the important point that developing and maintaining good emotional and mental discipline is the labour of a lifetime. Constructive thinking habits are something we all have to work at.

Masters of their universe

One of the striking features of Sally's narrative is that she sees herself as capable of remedying her situation by applying herself in future training sessions, whereas Aaron displays the characteristic 'learned helplessness' of a depressive personality.

Depressed people typically experience themselves as having very little control over their lives and there is an important overlap between these two states. To be depressed is, on one level, to feel out of control. This is probably why the behaviour of depressed boys in particular can so often resemble that of thwarted toddlers. When thinking about children's vulnerability to depression, it is probably important to recognize that being a child is a condition that involves more than its fair share of powerlessness.

Early childhood, especially, is a period of our lives when we have virtually no say about what happens to us. Most decisions are made on our behalf by our parents. Things happen to us that we do not want and that we would not choose. We are forced into clothes that sometimes do not feel comfortable, have food pushed into our mouths that we do not fancy, and find ourselves carted into a wide variety of situations at the whim of our carers.

For quite a long period we do not even enjoy control over our most basic bodily functions. This is maybe why, for toddlers, continence can often become such a political issue. It can be as a proud assertion of self-control or a weapon against the authority of others. In infancy we can do virtually nothing for ourselves. For all practical purposes we are completely helpless.

In infancy our helplessness is so extreme that I suspect most of the time (uncomfortable wet nappies and empty stomachs aside) this is probably scarcely an issue. It is when toddlers start to taste the possibility of control that the true extent of their relative powerlessness begins to sink in. This is often when the battles really begin between parents and their offspring. The 'terrible twos' is a rather optimistic euphemism for a campaign that often extends far beyond the third year of life – depending, of course, on the temperament of your child.

We all need to feel some degree of control over our lives. Rats put into an experimental condition in which electric shocks are administered to them in a random, unpredictable fashion soon become listless and make no efforts to safeguard themselves. They appear to 'give up', behaving just like depressed people. Conversely, when seeing clinically depressed patients one of the first steps taken by many therapists is to get their clients involved in 'activity scheduling'. This involves negotiating small, manageable goals that over time allow clients to recover some sense of themselves as effective, capable people who are not completely powerless.

Giving your children opportunities to master situations and use their talents is not just about making them into more rounded individuals: it is also an important protective measure against future mental health problems. Young children quite rightly take great pride in their accomplishments, and carers do well to create conditions in which children can experience the satisfactions of successfully completing challenges and acting more independently.

> Give your child some areas of control in her life. Allow her to make some choices: just not over everything.

There is, of course, a balance to be struck. For a child, having too much power can be just as stressful as having too little. Much has been written about the psychological difficulties of living in a modern world that overwhelms us with so many opportunities and choices on a daily basis. Children need to feel contained. They appear to sense that they are not yet equipped to manage themselves or their lives independently of their carers. Consequently, a child who has been given too much control within the family is seldom a happy one. A key skill of parenting is the ability to navigate this perilous border. This means encouraging a child's sense of autonomy without undermining his security – and the latter depends upon the child's perception that someone loving and competent is ultimately running the show.

Research suggests it is a good idea to encourage your child to make choices, develop competencies and function independently but always within sensible parameters. If you give your pre-school child *carte blanche* choice over what he wants to wear every day, get ready to trail round the supermarket each week in the company of an increasingly grubby Spiderman. And if you do create this expectation, make sure you prepare yourself for a 'Battle Royal' when the day comes when you do need him to wear something warmer or (in your view) more appropriate at his grandparents' golden wedding celebration.

On the other hand, giving a young child regular experience of more restricted either/or choices ('Do you want to wear your *red* jumper today, Callum, or the *blue* one?') fosters a sense of control at a level that is likely to prove acceptable to you and helpful for your child. Obviously, as your child grows towards his teenage years, he is able to take on a more significant level of control and personal responsibility, but the expansion needs to be gradual. Teenagers who are suddenly given a large measure of personal freedom without adequate preparation in earlier childhood can easily feel overwhelmed and are highly vulnerable to peer pressure.

> As your child gets older, gradually increase the amount of control they have over their own lives, making a gradual transition from toddlers' simple choices to late teenage independence.

As your child gets older, resist the temptation to keep your baby dependent on you. Teach the skills that will ultimately help her to function in life and view herself as a competent individual. You can enhance a child's sense of mastery enormously by teaching practical skills: how to cook, how to read a map, how to balance a bank account. Does your teenager know how to resuscitate someone, how to wire a plug or do his own ironing? We need to help our children develop a sure sense of themselves as capable individuals who can handle whatever life throws at them.

It's a great shame that many teenagers leave for college still unable to fend for themselves or even perform simple domestic tasks. Don't let your child join their ranks. If we allow our offspring to become passive and helpless we are also predisposing them towards a depressive mindset.

Giving them a leg up

In order to help children develop their sense of mastery parents need to operate sensitively in what the Russian psychologist Vygotsky called 'the zone of proximal development'. This may sound like something out of a sci-fi movie but the concept is a simple one. Vygotsky believed that children learn best when given appropriate support to help them accomplish tasks that lie just beyond their unaided reach. By helping to structure the task, or by directing the child's attention to relevant aspects of it, an adult can often help a child to reach the next level of ability. By gradually internalizing such 'scaffolding' experiences the child becomes more capable of performing similar tasks on her own.

For scaffolding to work effectively it is vital that the carer assists the child without 'taking over' or rushing ahead. Asking pertinent questions that will enable the child to find his own solutions is far more helpful to your child than providing him with the answers yourself. Drawing comparisons between aspects of the current task and relevant skills already in your child's repertoire can also be a productive strategy. Simply providing an interested commentary describing what you see your child doing may foster a level of self-awareness that can pave the way for a breakthrough.

In scaffolding your role is to act as a resource and support rather than teacher. Make occasional suggestions by all means if you sense that your child is becoming disheartened and frustrated but resist the temptation to do too much. If your child can successfully find his own way through a challenging task the rewards will be much sweeter and the resultant sense of achievement much greater.

> Give children tasks to do that are just out of their reach unaided, but possible with a little bit of guidance or advice: 'If you colour in the petals, I'll help you do the leaves ...'

'Praise you like I should ...'

When pitched appropriately, the right kind of praise can really help develop your child's sense of competence. When you praise your child try to avoid generalizations and focus on the specifics. Rather than simply enthuse about 'what a lovely painting' he has done, try and pick out aspects of it that you feel are worthy of special mention:

- 'I really like the way you have used all the different colours to create the sense of light coming through the leaves ...'

- 'It's brilliant how these figures here really look as if they are running across the park. How did you manage to make them look as if they are moving?'

- 'The amount of detail in your picture makes it really interesting to look at ... There's so much going on here, Robert – It's amazing!'

These kinds of observation not only let your child know that you are genuinely appreciative of the product, but also provide feedback that will help build and develop skills.

Discriminating praise is ultimately much more valuable to your child than pretending that everything he does is wonderful. There is a common misconception that constantly affirming children through praise is the royal road to self-esteem. However, positive psychology research stresses that a far more reliable foundation of self-esteem is the individual's personal experience of succeeding and mastering challenges, both great and small, throughout the course of life. To accomplish this your child will need honest, constructive feedback as well as your affirmation and encouragement.

> Give detailed feedback and constructive criticism rather than blanket praise.

Individuals who view themselves as competent and able to achieve their goals are more likely to feel good about themselves and be psychologically robust. Always let your child know that your love for them is unconditional. However, if your praise is too fulsome and always couched in generalities, the likelihood is that it will rapidly become a devalued currency for your children.

When you do offer praise, also keep the emphasis on the personal qualities that your child has shown or the skills he has employed, rather than just the outcome of his labours. You want to reinforce the attitudes and approaches that will enhance your child's ability to achieve future goals:

- 'I'm really impressed by how you have managed to stick with that maths homework, even when I know you felt like giving up ... But you got through it and now you won't have it hanging over you this weekend.'

- 'You have got so much more organized in the way you are approaching things these days, Charlie. I noticed how you laid all the ingredients out before you started making the cake which – by the way – is incredibly light and moist...'

- 'That five minutes you put into brainstorming ideas beforehand really paid off ... Your story is so imaginative. By the end I really wanted to know how it was going to work out...'

Attending to the process rather than just the outcome of their efforts also helps children to derive value from their sense of themselves as learners who are constantly expanding and developing their skills base. This stops them seeing themselves as people whose worth depends solely upon what they can achieve.

Finally, as your child develops a taste for mastery, so she will learn to place greater value on the mental skills and attitudes needed to expand it. Very few worthwhile challenges can be successfully accomplished without tolerating frustration, subduing impulses and delaying immediate gratification. As you provide a child with opportunities to control the world around him you are also reinforcing the rewards of controlling himself and helping him practise these essential skills.

We have already noted that the parts of the brain involved in planning, co-ordinating and focusing activity are precisely the same regions that are involved in emotional regulation. Exercising this mental muscle in a context in which the rewards are so motivating will have the added benefit of making your child more able to manage turbulence in his emotional life. This, in turn, should give him greater control over his behaviour.

Promoting mindfulness

One of the most exciting recent developments in the modern treatment of depression has been the integration of cognitive behavioural principles with insights from an eastern tradition that goes back many thousands of years.

The practice of 'mindfulness' is a form of meditation that emphasizes closing down depressive thinking by paying attention only to the present moment and accepting the contents of your thoughts. Rather than striving to change the contents of your thoughts overtly, the practitioners of the mindfulness approach develop the capacity to 'bear witness' to them in a relaxed, non-judgemental fashion. Those who develop this discipline are often able to break the stranglehold of the depressed mind state.

Psychologists have sought to understand why the mindfulness approach can be so effective. They believe that one of the main drivers of a depressive mindset is obsessive 'discrepancy analysis' – in other words a preoccupation with the seemingly insurmountable gap between where you are and where you would like to be. Their suggestion is that the mindfulness approach short-circuits this painful and counterproductive process of comparison by not attempting to change the present or look beyond it, but to accept it for what it is, even if it is distressing or unpleasant.

The reality is that our experience changes moment by moment but, as we have already seen, a depressed person will usually ignore or edit out anything that might prove neutral or even uplifting. The practice of mindfulness keeps the individual open to experience in a way that runs counter to the habits of a depressed mind. It stops people getting caught up in cycles of negative thinking by holding everything lightly and helping them to become observers of their own thoughts rather than their slaves.

Research evidence shows that the practice of mindfulness really can help reduce relapse amongst depressed adults, and it's likely that the key attitudes also underpin a mentally healthy outlook.

We can certainly encourage our children to develop some of the hallmarks of mindfulness. Learning to concentrate, to really observe and live in the present is a talent that has to be developed. It starts with learning to still the babbling of busy young minds, and bringing attention back to the job in hand. The modern world leaves us in a constantly over-stimulated state: we are awash with a barrage of information from the media and the internet; our lives consist of constantly changing priorities and roles.

> Encourage your child to concentrate and ignore distractions, to really observe and live in the present.

Because we have got used to dealing with constant flux and so many competing demands, the simplicity and focus of doing one thing at a time is becoming quite alien to us. If the level of stimulation drops below the cultural norm, many children feel ill at ease. Teach your children to be as comfortable with simplicity and silence as they are with the pyrotechnics of the multimedia age.

No one is designed to multi-task all the time. How is your child to learn to attend to the flavours and textures of food if every meal is accompanied by the distraction of the TV set? Take your child out into nature and train her to observe: point out detail, examine the intricate veins on the back of a leaf, the ridges on shells or the glistening trails left by the snails. Stand on a hillside together, close your eyes together and see whether you can concentrate on listening, really listening, for a whole minute. Start doing these things while your child is young and you will be encouraging good mental hygiene in later life.

> Take your child outside and let her study the tiniest details of nature. Help her learn to be comfortable with simplicity and silence.

It is a shame that the art of collecting things is becoming so neglected. Whether it be stamps, character cards or bottle tops, pouring over a prized collection trained children to focus their attention in a way not encouraged by the fast-moving world of DVDs and computer games.

I am sounding like an old fogy but I make no apology. The latest health research is telling us that the ability to live fully in the moment and develop a quality of sustained attention has genuine protective value for all of us.

The 17th century French moralist Jean de la Bruyère claimed that 'children have neither past nor future; they enjoy the present'. However, while children may have an innate talent for 'living in the moment' we need to remember that life has changed, making it difficult to hang on to this valuable ability. If we are serious about protecting our children's mental health we may need to work a little harder if we want our children to be able to swim upstream against the constant distractions of modern life.

 ## Quick summary action points

- Be aware that depressed states of mind are often responsible for bad behaviour in children.

- Learn to spot and challenge characteristic features of a depressed mindset:
  —Bad events will be interpreted as *permanent, far-reaching* and *person-related*.
  —Good events will be regarded as *temporary, localized* and a product of *external* factors.

- Nurture your child's sense of mastery to ward off 'learned helplessness':
  —Provide opportunities to meet challenges and develop practical skills.
  —Offer a young child controlled choices, for example, by making use of either–or alternatives.
  —Develop your child's sense of control through effective scaffolding.

- Use discriminating praise:
  —Be specific about the merits of what your child has done.
  —Focus on the process as well as the product: affirm attitudes, qualities and strategies that will ensure future success.

- Help your child develop a 'mindful' approach towards life:
  - —Create periods at home when distractions are kept to a minimum.
  - —Avoid constant multi-tasking and help your child learn to pay attention to detail.
  - —Foster a taste for stillness and simplicity.

5
Wrestling with monsters

Overcoming stress and anxiety

'Sometimes I just lie there and so many things are in my mind I find it really hard to get to sleep. You know when a plane lands at night and you look out of the window and you see this big spider's web of twinkling lights? Well that's what it's like in my head. Each of those little lights is a different worry ... If I zoom in on one of them its like when the plane gets close to the ground and you can only see a few of the lights at a time – but the rest are still out there somewhere. When you are that close up you can't see the others any more. But they're still there.'

James (10 years old)

We can all be seduced by a vision of childhood as an endless summer of carefree, cloudless skies and dreamless nights. Perhaps this is because we so badly want it to be like this for our own kids. Or maybe because we need to believe that there is an alternative to the demanding, cynical world we often inhabit as adults? Whatever the reason, we cannot afford to pretend that our children are growing up in a protected bubble. These days, children have to cope with many of the same pressures of modern life as the rest of us. And, just like us, sometimes they struggle. Unfortunately, when children are not coping well with the stress in their lives it can have a dramatic impact upon their behaviour.

Understanding what causes stress in children and giving them tools to deal with anxiety, is one of the most valuable investments parents can make in their future well-being. It is one of the fundamental skills upon which children's ability to regulate their behaviour depends.

How stress affects us

Stress and aggression go hand in hand. As we all know from school biology lessons, when our backs are against the wall our minds and bodies prepare us to do one of two things: namely run away or come out fighting. This is a mechanism that has served our species well since prehistoric times. It prevented our ancestors ending up as hors-d'oeuvres for all manner of scary Jurassic predators. However, it also means that under stress people of all ages are primed to attack. The 'cooling' mechanisms that usually restrain antisocial behaviour have less purchase, because in crisis mode we are programmed to give priority to the rapid-response survival circuits of the primitive brain. The brakes are off.

We can all recognize how much more easily we are provoked when stressed. As adults even low-level background stress can leave us cranky and irritable, and prone to biting the heads off friends, family and colleagues. Under acute stress some people become physically violent. In rare circumstances, extreme stress can cause reasonable people to act in completely irrational ways that have devastating consequences.

If such things can happen to adults, with their fully developed frontal lobes and years of self-restraint practice, how much more vulnerable are children to the effects that anxiety can have upon their behaviour? Before shaking our heads in despair at the 'ASBO generation' perhaps we should pause to consider the role played by chronic stress both in the extremes of antisocial behaviour and the more commonplace tantrums of our own little angels.

Natural-born stress heads?

Susceptibility to stress varies enormously between children. Over recent years much work has been done to map the findings of research into personality onto the insights of scientists more directly concerned with the physiology and biology of the brain.

Of all the aspects of personality that have been used to measure differences between people, the trait of neuroticism has proved one of the most reliable. It has taken its rightful place amongst the 'Big Five' – the key dimensions of personality in which researchers now have the most confidence. People who score highly on neuroticism are born worriers. Like Woody Allen who once remarked, 'I am not afraid to die; I just don't want to be there when it happens,' neurotic individuals are, by definition, highly vulnerable to stress.

Psychologist Daniel Nettle suggests that the features associated with neuroticism can best be summarized by heightened sensitivity to negative feelings of all kinds. This is supported by the fact that people who suffer from full-blown anxiety disorders such as phobias, obsessive compulsive disorder and post-traumatic stress are more likely to score highly on this trait.

We are beginning to achieve a better understanding of the biology behind these tendencies. For instance, the amygdala (seat of the primitive, emotion-driven brain) seems to be more active and even bigger and denser in people who score highly on neuroticism measures. Physical differences also show up in their prefrontal cortex – in precisely the area that usually lights up on a scan when people need to suppress negative reactions.

The psychiatrist and researcher Klaus Peter-Lesch has discovered that high neuroticism scorers are also more likely to be carrying a short form of a piece of genetic code known as the serotonin transporter gene. As the neuro-transmitter most closely identified with soothing anxious and depressed states of mind serotonin plays a key role in Mother Nature's technology for 'kissing it better'. Drugs like Prozac are thought to work (although who knows these days?) by preventing serotonin from being reab-sorbed by brain cells. The calming effects of physical exercise are also probably due to their effect on the brain's serotonergic pathways. The good news for many of us is that chocolate also affects the nervous system in much the same way. It's a hard call.

Such findings do suggest that some people are naturally biased towards neuroticism and the high levels of anxiety that go with it. If your child is amongst them then the advice in this chapter is especially relevant. However, even the most mellow of us has our limits and no child is immune to the eroding effects that stress can have on rea-sonable behaviour.

The hallmarks of a stressed child

'I swear he's possessed ...' complained the mother of 6-year-old Harry. 'He has been in a foul mood for most of the week and yesterday I found him in his sister's room cheerfully disembowelling her toy cat with a kitchen knife. The stuffing was flying everywhere. But the moment I went into the room he looks up at me with these big helpless eyes (the knife still in his hand, mind you) and yells: "It wasn't me!" Then suddenly his face crumples up and he starts howling . . . His father keeps asking when his period's due!'

What Harry's mother was describing is fairly typical of a child under duress and it was no great surprise to discover that Harry's behaviour was most likely a delayed reaction to a recent house move. Abrupt mood swings, lying and bullying behaviour can all be the outward signs of internal pressure as your child's powers of self-control break down. For the reasons already mentioned, stressed children may also report finding it difficult to concentrate and may become more forgetful than usual.

When stress hormone levels are elevated they can also produce some of the physical symptoms of anxiety: feeling out of breath, trembly or dizzy. Your child may appear to be 'going down with something', complaining of pins and needles, headaches, stomach cramps or feeling suddenly hot or cold. Increased sweating may leave the skin clammy to the touch and the psychological effects of these hormones can make your child feel unsettled and strange. Sleep patterns can also be disrupted and your child may start having nightmares – even if the content of these appears to be unrelated to anything going on in your child's everyday life.

If your child is ever unfortunate enough to suffer a full blown panic attack these symptoms may increase in intensity to the point that both you and your child may fear that there is something seriously physically wrong. In the throes of a panic attack people can suffer from palpitations, loss of feeling in their limbs, choking sensations and disorientation. They experience intense fear that they are going mad or even about to die. In fact, although acutely disturbing when they occur, the symptoms of panic attacks are physically harmless. However, if things are this bad your child may require professional help and you should talk to your GP.

As far as anxiety responses within the 'normal' range are concerned, you should also be on the look out for signs of regressive behaviour. Anxious children may 'turn back the clock' emotionally by resorting to habits and long out-grown patterns of behaviour like sucking their thumb or wanting to keep you in sight at all times. Older children are more likely to become defiant and objectionable, surly, rude and withdrawn.

Before we look at some techniques your child can use to combat anxious thinking, it is worth becoming aware of the sorts of things that cause children to become stressed. Although they overlap with adult concerns, some of them are specific to children and may not even be immediately obvious to our adult eyes.

Is the news bad news for children?

Many children get very concerned about current affairs. In moderation, television can be a great source of education and entertainment for kids. But unrestricted viewing also confronts children with realities many of them are not psychologically ready to digest: even pre-watershed they will witness scenes of violence and bloodshed, see starving and abandoned children from all over the world, and hear reports of children being abducted from hotel rooms while they sleep.

Listen to the questions children ask and you will be left

in little doubt about the undercurrent of anxiety that exposure to the media can stir up: 'Can our house flood like those ones on the news?', 'If there was a war in our country would you have to go and fight, Daddy?', 'What will happen to Pez [the family dog] when the sun burns up the earth?', 'When will I get cancer like that girl with no hair?'

In the mid 1990s I was a junior researcher in a government-funded study that was following a group of children from infancy into their teenage years. Part of my job was to interview them and their parents about various aspects of their lives. The children were eight years old when I went to see them but I distinctly remember being constantly surprised by how many parents said their children had nightmares about current affairs stories they had heard on the news or seen on TV.

It is all too easy to leave the television on in the background, with the result that we may not even be conscious of what our children are taking in. Unfortunately, children often lack the information, experience or understanding to put news stories into context or assess risks realistically. Because of this, children tend to fill in the gaps with their imagination. An eye-catching headline can provide the seed for vivid nightmare scenarios that can later keep them awake at night.

If you are going to allow your child to watch the news, I would suggest that until your child reaches double figures you restrict viewing to current affairs programmes aimed at a younger audience. Also, it can be helpful to make this an activity where you and your child sit down and watch together. Firstly, you will know exactly what he has seen and, more importantly, you will be able to review the content of the programme with him. In this way you have an opportunity to tackle any fears and offer a more balanced perspective.

Don't be afraid to ask younger children directly whether they have concerns about anything they have seen on the screen so you know how to respond. You will also be encouraging a family culture in which your child gets used to voicing their fears. This is particularly important in light of a recent Kidscape survey reporting that only a quarter of 9–13 year olds were prepared to share their worries with a parent.

> If you let your under-10 year old watch the news, be there with them and ask if there's anything they've seen that bothers them.

If your child does confide a fear about something they have seen or heard, always take it seriously. Resist the temptation to 'laugh it off' or dismiss it out of hand. This won't make your child feel any better. Children can get anxious about things that may seem absurd to grown-ups, but if they feel ridiculed they may well decide to keep their concerns to themselves in future. Many of our own fears are irrational, but that does not make them any less real. Giving your child's anxieties thoughtful consideration and adopting a pragmatic, problem-solving approach is helpful at a number of levels. Not only does it demonstrate that you are engaging with his concerns, but also shows your child that a rational, reasoned response can go a long way to setting his mind at ease.

> Never ever laugh off a child's anxiety – however silly it may seem to you. Always give a thoughtful, rational response.

Schoolwork stress

In my clinical work I come across more and more children who are severely stressed about how they are doing at school, and these children are just the tip of the iceberg. Recent surveys confirm that academic performance is a pressing source of concern for many children: fears about not doing well at school are often linked to anxieties about their future prospects once they leave. As one perfectly able eight year old confided to me through floods of tears: 'I am not the brightest in the class ... I am bound to get a *really* bad job.' That children as young as this boy should be thinking this way is terribly sad, but as parents we need to recognize that the pressure children experience in this area feels very real. Rightly or wrongly, a surprising number of children are convinced that without the right qualifications they stand little chance of achieving a secure foothold upon an uncertain future.

Of course many parents share this belief and the anxiety that goes with it. Fear is a highly contagious emotion and it is all too easy for parents and children to infect each other and create a destructive, anxious atmosphere around the whole issue of homework and academic performance.

I am not implying that good grades and qualifications are unimportant or that we shouldn't do everything we can to help our children fulfil their academic potential. However, we do need to hold out against the extreme anxiety-inducing position in many children's minds that *everything* depends upon how well they do at school. For a start this is simply not true. Increasingly the evidence suggests that the cluster of non-academic qualities that make up emotional intelligence are far more likely to determine an individual's long-term prospects. Many of our nation's most successful people left school with very meagre qualifications – or none at all.

> Don't let your child believe that success at school is the *only* thing that matters in life – or that a highly paid job is the only aim.

In any case, we also need to help children challenge the idea that a highly paid job is the only job worth having. While a powerful advertising industry promotes the idea that acquisition is the key to contentment, all the positive psychology research into happiness suggests that an increase in income is only correlated with life satisfaction up to a certain, quite modest level. Beyond that point it makes no difference. The old saying is true: 'Money (well lots of it anyway) really cannot buy you happiness.' We all want our children to be happy, but we also need to make sure that we are instilling values and priorities that are genuinely going to promote quality of life.

On a purely practical level, if we put children under too much pressure to succeed we actually make it harder for them to do their best. Psychologists have known for a long time that chronic stress makes it harder to think and concentrate. Rather unfairly, if you are already feeling under pressure at school, this is a side-effect likely to make life even more stressful for you, especially in a classroom setting. We are now beginning to understand a little more about the way in which stress affects the brain.

Cortisol is one of the main stress hormones. It is designed to shock the body into battle readiness and it does a very efficient job. But in a threatening situation in which there is no appropriate fight or flight response to neutralize cortisol levels, it stays in the bloodstream longer than it should.

The hippocampus is an area of the brain that plays a key role in memory and the co-ordination of information and it appears to be particularly sensitive to the effects of stress hormones. In some people with chronically elevated cortisol levels signs of physical damage even show up on scan. One study found that the hippocampus in brains of adult Vietnamese subjects suffering from post-traumatic stress disorder (a condition that bathes the brain in cortisol over long periods) appeared to have shrunk by up to 26 per cent. The impact that stress may have on the developing brain of children is not yet fully understood but findings such as these do not bode well.

Of course not all stress is bad for you or your child. Children need to be put into situations that challenge, excite and extend them. Occasional, controlled exposure to stress can improve their performance in some settings. However, generally high stress levels are not helpful and can significantly undermine children's performance at school.

Continual assessment means that many children (and their parents) experience the sustained pressure of trying to achieve high marks for every piece of marked coursework. Stress in a more acute form comes from formal tests and exams, when younger children can also become very stressed. However sensitively they are administered, children are fully aware that their ability is being measured, and for some of them this is highly anxiety-provoking. Sadly, children have a tendency to believe that it is not just their reading age or numeracy that is being graded but their worth as people.

For dealing with anxieties about school performance many of the techniques for dealing with anxious thoughts covered later in this chapter are relevant. However, for parents the following suggestions may be helpful:

- Try and stay relaxed yourself. Remember that children develop at different rates, especially in the early years. However, if you are worried about your child's performance at school then be proactive: make an appointment to discuss your concerns with the relevant teacher who will be able to give you accurate feedback and make suggestions as to how you can best support your child's learning.

- Keep the channels of communication with your child open. Be sensitive to periods during which he may feel under pressure and give him opportunities to talk about his fears. However, also respect the fact that a stressed child may not always want to talk and at times like these find practical ways to remind him of your love and support. Home baking always worked for me.

- If your child is overly anxious about performance, work through her catastrophic beliefs about the implications of not doing well at school. Help her challenge negative thoughts that her worth as a person or future prospects hinge entirely on her grades, or that a low mark on a maths test means she will be living in a shop doorway later in life.

- Do not make your approval dependent upon achievement. By all means express pride in your child's accomplishments, but focus your praise on the qualities and attitudes that helped him do well: his dedication, his focus, his hard work. Always emphasize the importance of fulfilling personal potential over being the best. Sooner or later your child will meet someone brighter, faster and more able.

- Make an effort to affirm the value of your child's achievements outside of schoolwork. Celebrate her skill on the football pitch, her comic timing, the fact that your neighbours now consider her responsible enough to babysit for them.

- Teach children to see 'failure' or low grades as useful feedback and part of an ongoing learning process that will help them develop. Cultivate what Carol Dweck calls a 'growth mindset' in which all setbacks are viewed as learning opportunities. Emphasize that ability is not fixed but can always be developed through practice.

- Concentrate on developing skills that will enable your child to feel more in control of his own learning. (For more information on these 'meta-skills', see Chapter 7.) Also help your child organize her schoolwork efficiently so that she can protect periods of free time during which she can relax and 'switch off' from the demands of school.

Taking it personally

'WHAT'S *WRONG* WITH YOU?!? JUST STOP GOING ON AT ME, YOU BITCH!' screams 11-year-old Jason, slamming the door on his bemused mother who has innocently suggested that he should think about getting his hair cut if he wants it to stop flopping in his eyes. Furious at overhearing his father informing a family friend that he has been feeling 'a bit poorly' that morning, 4-year-old Duncan suddenly howls in protest: 'I **MORE** THAN A LITTLE BIT POORLY!' His trembling indignation is palpable, even down the phone.

Looking at these examples you may well be wondering what on earth is going on here? Jason certainly crossed a line in speaking so abusively towards his mother, but the real question is why did these two boys react so strongly to such innocuous remarks?

The answer probably has something to do with a source of tension in childhood that often lies well hidden beneath the surface – namely the underlying fragility of many children's sense of self.

'Hold on a minute . . .' you object, 'This doesn't sound like the voice of self-doubt to me. Surely, what the Jasons and Duncans of this world need is to be taken down a peg or two?' I agree that Jason's abusive comments are unacceptable and demand a robust response. However, if we ignore the psychological dynamics driving this kind of behaviour we could end up targeting the symptom rather than the cause.

The term 'primary narcissicism' refers to a perfectly normal phase of development. It describes periods when children can become especially self-centred, demanding and completely unable to tolerate things being other than precisely the way they want them. You often see it most prominently in toddlers but it can re-emerge once more during the teenage years. Narcissists, whether young or old, can be pretty tiresome company. Prickly if criticised, they carry around with them a dramatically inflated sense of their importance in the scheme of things. However obnoxious, what needs to be recognized is that underneath all the bravado and arrogance, the narcissist is overcompensating for a gnawing insecurity.

Deep down all narcissists are trying to protect themselves from feelings of shame. They question the ability of the world to meet their needs and much of their energy is devoted to monitoring and protecting their brittle identities. Being constantly on the defensive like this is inevitably stressful, and makes narcissistic people of all ages hypersensitive to criticism. Even constructive feedback or the most innocent of suggestions can be experienced as a personal assault for a child still feeling her way towards a secure sense of self.

We all anchor our identities by emotionally investing in things. These might include an important relationship, a job, a particular talent or even possessions such as a favourite jacket, a CD collection or, in Jason's case, a particular look or hairstyle. We feel these things represent us and say something important about who we are. If they are taken from us, we feel diminished. As we get older we usually become less reliant on these external symbols of self, but children who do not yet know who they are can be highly dependent upon them and feel very threatened if theirs are tampered with. This is partly why so many toddlers find it so hard to share their toys, and why adolescents fight so ferociously with their parents about body piercings, skirt lengths and tidy bedrooms.

> Be aware of things that children have strong emotional attachments to. This includes other people or possessions or even parts of their body. Any criticism of those things can be devastating to children.

It is important that parents recognize how exposed children can feel during these stages of their development. The background stress generated in their lives is considerable. As the parent, to some extent you may have to grit your teeth and endure your child's heightened tetchiness during such phases. However, there are a few things you can do to make life less stressful for both of you.

- Where possible, do tread carefully round your child's symbols of self, even if she has made investments that seem trivial or alien to you. Pick your battles wisely.

- Check that there is a valid reason for asking your child to do what you request. You do not always have to explain yourself but if your child can manipulate you to the point at which you fall back on 'Because I say so!' then in her own head she has exposed your nurturing as naked power play. This merely confirms her fears that she needs to be on guard against you in future.

- Acknowledge how your child might be feeling – but be careful not to put words into his mouth.

- If your child is overly sensitive to criticism try and use open questions to help her draw her own conclusions about what she might need to learn to ensure a better outcome in future.

All change

For many young children different equals bad. Remember the last time you washed your child's comforter? Or served up something unfamiliar for lunch? Even such minor alterations are remarkably unsettling for some children.

Whoever devised the saying 'A change is as good as a rest' failed to recognize the mental and emotional demands that change can place on us. Change can indeed revitalize us, but in novel situations in which we can no longer fall back upon established routines the results can be psychologically taxing. It is no coincidence that the top 10 stressors for adults all relate to significant life transitions: the death of a spouse; the ending of a relationship; moving house. Even as grown-ups the amount of change that we can cope with comfortably is limited. It can be great to go on holiday and visit new places, take in new sights and sample a different cuisine, but few of us do not feel some sense of relief when we step back through our own front door.

Considering how much change children have to manage in the course of their brief lives, it is not surprising that they are wary of it. In the early years their bodies morph continually, their abilities expand exponentially and their routines are in a constant state of flux. There is so much to learn, so many skills to acquire, that few things in a child's life ultimately remain consistent. Even within their families over a third of them will have experienced a separation or divorce by the time they are 16.

Most parents will already be aware of events commonly associated with childhood stress. Death, separation and divorce, the illness of a parent or close relative – such life events can have a powerful effect on some children. However, it is important to recognize that even positive changes can raise stress levels for many children.

Six-year-old Craig and his mother had recently been rehoused by the council. Their new home was a spacious flat that allowed Craig to have his own bedroom for the first time. Craig loved the new flat and told me proudly about how the walls of his new room had been freshly lined with posters of his rugby-playing heroes. Nevertheless he was also confused by how anxious he felt in his new environment. Although it was indisputably better, it just didn't feel the *same* as the old place with its noisy neighbours and rattling windows.

When told that it was perfectly normal to feel this way and that it might take time to get used to the new flat Craig looked enormously relieved. 'I just felt bad...' he explained, 'I didn't want my mum to think I didn't like where we are now because I *really* do. I just don't quite know myself there yet...'

In Craig's case, simply reassuring him that his reaction to change was entirely normal did a lot to ease the pressure he was feeling. If you know your child is facing changes of any kind, whether to do with shifting allegiances within friendship groups or being moved between maths sets, be aware that he may be more stressed than he acknowledges. On the other hand, if your son or daughter's behaviour starts falling apart, one of the first questions to ask yourself (and them) is whether anything in their world has altered recently.

- If you know that a significant change is on the horizon give your child a chance to prepare. The more information you provide, the more she can picture herself in her new circumstances and get used to the idea. For example, if your child has to go into hospital for treatment take her into the ward, arrange for her to meet the staff and talk to someone who has been through the same procedure. Let her ask questions and run through exactly what will happen when she goes in. Rather than feeding anxiety, in most cases access to knowledge gives children back a sense of control.

- Present your child with a realistic picture of what will happen. Don't be tempted to gloss over the difficulties or focus exclusively on the benefits.

- With your child, brainstorm the implications of any big change – both positive and negative – in terms of the impact it may have on her life. Draw up a list of pros and cons.

- Recognize that change often involves an element of loss. Allow your child to experience and express his feelings about it without censoring them. There may be a process of letting go that he needs to work through, so give him time.

- Acknowledge the stress involved in change and that most changes in children's lives are orchestrated by other people. Sometimes simply recognizing this can diffuse the tension children feel.

- If possible, give your child an active role in any changes that affect her. It can be helpful for older siblings to be given responsibilities in helping look after a new baby or for an older child to start picking out paint colours for his new room in anticipation of a house move.

- Make clear what will *not* change, and identify any relevant skills that your child is taking with him into the new situation: 'I know it is not the same, Max, but you will still be able to see your friends from your old school at weekends and in the holidays. You will no doubt carry on chatting to them at all hours via the computer. It can be hard at first in a new school when you don't know anyone yet but ever since your first day at nursery I have always been impressed by how good you are at making new friends. Not everyone can do that.'

- Do give your child opportunities to discuss the change with you and raise any related worries. Sometimes children can get worked up quite needlessly. I know of one child who had assumed that when his family moved to a new town they would be leaving the cat behind (which was not in fact the case) and another who thought that once his much-loved granddad moved into the retirement home he would no longer be allowed to visit.

> Help children prepare for change – however small or large – and anticipate it being difficult for them. Give them the chance to talk over their worries.

Too much stimulation ... or too little?

At wedding receptions you are likely to find two kinds of child tucked away under the banquet table. The first is usually accompanied by a bright-eyed, giggling cousin as the pair revels in the illicit thrill of stolen champagne or other contraband. For the second the cool folds of the table cloth offer a temporary sanctuary from the noise, bustle and business of the whole occasion.

Psychologists have known for years that people feel comfortable with different levels of stimulation. Just as the thermostat on your central heating turns the boiler off when it gets too hot or fires the system up when the temperature drops below its setting, so we all tend to adjust our environment to keep levels of stimulation within the range that suits us.

People who like to keep the stimulation setting high are the extroverts. These are the outgoing, 24-hour party animals whose high-octane lifestyle feeds their need for sensation and excitement. At the other end of the spectrum are the extreme introverts who are more likely to be found curled up on the sofa with a glass of wine and a good book of an evening.

Such differences are hard-wired into the brain and are linked to the way that the brain responds to arousal. They do not mean that introverts *never* want to let their hair down or that extroverts never stand still. However, the contrasting lifestyles of high-scoring introverts and extroverts is some indication of how driven we are to keep our general level of arousal within the range that suits us.

When we are not able to do this we become stressed. In fact, the stress response is one of the feedback mechanisms that lets us know we are out of our stimulation comfort zone. Most of us are already aware that over-stimulation can have a powerful effect on children. Attend any children's birthday party and you can witness the results for yourself. For every wild child jumping on your sofa or trying to sling jelly across the room, there will be tear-stained casualties for whom the whole event is proving just too much. However, we are less tuned into the fact that when the stimulation level drops below what we require this can be equally stressful for us.

> Too much or too little stimulation can be bad for children. All children need and want different levels of action and quiet. Get to know your child – and help her get to know herself.

Boredom is difficult to tolerate, and many children find it unbearable. Most of us recognize that an over-stimulated child is likely to have trouble managing his behaviour but the same can also be said of an under-stimulated one. One of the first steps that a dog trainer will take with a disobedient or aggressive dog is to make sure that the animal is getting adequate exercise. Under-stimulated children will resort to desperate measures to get their arousal level back into a more temperate range. You can see this in the way that children strapped into the back of a car for long periods resort to bickering with each other in an attempt to up the level of excitement in the immediate environment. Alternatively they may try and provoke you with a relentless round of 'Are-we-there-yet?' style interrogation.

As your child gets older it is useful to help her understand where she lies on the introvert-extrovert scale and what that means in terms of warding off the stress that accompanies too little or too much stimulation. Once your child reaches the age of seven she can take one of the online, child-friendly personality tests like the Murphy–Meisgeier Type Indicator for Children (a children's version of the famous Myers-Briggs test) which will give her some sense of how much stimulation she needs. Try http://www.capt.org/assessment-mmtic for the Meisgeier for 7 upwards or parents can fill in the California Child Q-Set (CCQ) for free at http://www.personalitylab.org (Understand your Child) to find out about their child's personality at an even younger age.

Teach your child to recognize when he needs to do something active, interesting or exciting, and when his internal stress sensors are telling him it is time to take things down a step. Some of the relaxation techniques described below are useful tools that can enable an over-stimulated child to restore his equilibrium.

Alternatively, make sure that your child also has a range of suitable activities available so that he can increase stimulation levels when necessary. Ideally these need to be things that do not always require your involvement or supervision. Many parents end up being blackmailed by their bored children into a constant round of extravagant trips and outings which are fine once in a while, but cannot be the staple solution to periods when your child needs to up her stimulation levels.

Basic sports equipment like footballs, skipping ropes and pogo sticks are ideal for children who crave physical stimulation. Many parents swear that a big garden trampoline is a worthwhile investment for such purposes – and a potentially entertaining one for adults once the kids are in bed.

Don't forget that novelty is also stimulating for children. Consider putting together a filing box of special projects for such times – this could contain recipes of things you and your child could cook together, instructions for a treasure hunt, or maybe a challenge to make three musical instruments out of household objects. There are many books available full of suitable suggestions.

In the children's story series *My Naughty Little Sister* there is a brilliant idea that could easily be copied. While convalescing, the little sister is given access to a special box of treasures assembled by a friendly neighbour. The box contains a series of intriguing but everyday items – a beautiful shell, a paper fan, a miniature doll. Each treasure is individually wrapped and packed in a compartment of a special chest. The reason why the box keeps the story's heroine so happily occupied is because it only comes out on rare occasions. Its contents consequently retain an aura of special fascination.

Whether or not you make your own treasure chest, the principle of holding back a selection of toys or games that are only brought out on selective occasions is a good one. It can provide a really useful resource for when bored children need stimulation. Many of today's children are completely deluged with gifts at Christmas and birthdays. Why not increase your child's enjoyment and their impact by staggering access to them through the year? If you introduce this principle early on your kids will never know anything different. In retrospect, I wish I had adopted this policy with my two.

> Have some toys and games that are not brought out frequently and/or give your children new toys or games regularly throughout the year, rather than all at once on their birthdays.

Facing your fear!

In this and the next section we will look at some simple techniques you can teach your child to help tackle the anxious thinking that can easily erode acceptable behaviour.

With all fears and phobias one of the keys to getting past them is helping children to stop avoiding what they fear.

You will remember from the cognitive model that thoughts, feelings and behaviour can all influence each other. Every time we avoid what we fear we are giving our brains the message that we are 'keeping ourselves safe'. Since it stands to reason that we only need to keep ourselves safe from things that are hazardous, our self-protective behaviour actually reinforces our sense of danger.

This is exactly what happened to 8-year-old Timothy. Ever since some friends in Halloween costume had surprised him on the doorstep he had become so terrified of masks that he could not walk past the fancydress shops in his local town without breaking out in a sweat. As a result he kept himself away from anything associated with masks and monsters and his phobia was becoming more and more limiting for him.

Tim was helped to confront his fears using a very basic technique called graded exposure. The first stage was to help him create his personal 'ladder of fear'. This consisted of a list of mask-related experiences and tasks that he thought would range from being mildly anxiety-provoking to absolutely terrifying for him. At the bottom end of Tim's hierarchy were items like simply talking about masks, then looking at pictures of non-Halloween masks until at the top of his list was the prospect of walking into one of the costume shops and handling a zombie mask.

Over the weeks we worked through the stages from the bottom up. At each stage Timothy found that after an initial peak in his anxiety levels his fears would subside. His mind was slowly re-educating itself: nothing bad was happening and with help he was able to keep himself in a more relaxed state. Gradually the 'frightening' experiences were being re-classified as safe. Moreover, Tim was learning that his predictions about how frightening a particular stage would be were not always accurate. Within a few weeks he was able to walk into the fancydress shop and handle a truly horrible-looking latex mask without great difficulty.

If you do use this approach with your own child, make sure that you have enough stages in your hierarchy, that you have been specific about each different stage and that the elements appear in the right order from easiest to most difficult. When you work your way through make sure your child has achieved a calm, controlled state at each level before moving on. Otherwise the whole thing will backfire. It is also important that you are able to demonstrate each step yourself in a collected, relaxed fashion. If you have a phobia of spiders yourself, you may not be the right person to help your child with his – unless, of course, you have already successfully completed a suitable desensitization programme yourself.

> If your child is frightened of something, help her face her fear by breaking it down into a series of manageable steps.

What if?

Anxiety paints a future full of frightening possibilities. Anxious thinking often ends up formulated in children's heads as a list of fearful questions: 'What if my mummy doesn't get better?', 'What if I fail my GCSEs?', 'What if everyone laughs at my braces?' While these questions are valid ones children gripped by fear seldom provide themselves with realistic answers. When children watch TV monsters through a crack in their fingers they are obeying two seemingly contradictory laws of fear: law one – 'Avoid the thing that frightens you'; law two – 'Keep what frightens you in sight at all times'. These 'What if' thoughts also allow a child to keep half an eye on his fears while preventing himself from taking in the whole picture.

A terrifying prospect is like a movie film in which the frame usually freezes at the point when the anxiety becomes overwhelming. Children become fixated, finding it hard to move the film on beyond the paralyzing image of the crowd of jeering faces, the dreaded results envelope, the awful moment when they stand on that stage and cannot remember their next line. Their fear tells them that these events would be unbearable and that they would have no way of coping. This is rarely the case. One of the ways in which you can help a child deal with such fears is to encourage her to look squarely at the worst-case scenario and replace the question 'What if …?' with the question 'What then …?'

Alisha is a shy 9-year-old with a vivid imagination. Over recent weeks she has become uncharacteristically sullen and moody. Last Tuesday she was found in the shopping mall with a couple of her friends when she should have been at school. For her mother, this is the last straw and she has brought Alisha for counselling.

When I ask Alisha if anything has been bothering her recently she eventually tells me that she has overheard her parents fighting almost every evening for the past week. Notice how the conversation is steered to help Alisha confront her fears while also exploring what resources she has available to cope with her worst-case scenario.

Me: So your Mum and Dad are arguing quite a lot then?

Alisha: Yes.

Me: Well there could be lots of reasons for that. But what do you think it means?

Alisha: Well they obviously can't stand the sight of each other if they can't be in the same room without shouting at each other all the time.

Me: Okay – well that is certainly one possibility. But if you're right *what is the worst thing about that?*

Alisha: It's how it always starts, isn't it?

Me: How what starts?

Alisha: You know ... [she stares down at the floor and looks angry] How long will this take?

Me: Look, I appreciate this is really hard to think about, Alisha, but if you can just stick with it I want to see if we can help you feel a bit less frightened. Rather than trying to push it out of your mind *let's think together about the **very** worst thing that could happen.* What are you picturing in your head?

Alisha: That they split up of course.

Me: Alright. Let's pretend you're right. *What would happen then?*

Alisha: Well my life would be spoilt. It would be horrible.

Me: I imagine you might feel very unhappy. *But what would happen then?*

Alisha: I would be sad for ever.

Me: For ever? Even when you are a grown up?

Alisha: Yes – even then. Well ... for a *really* long time anyway.

Me: Hmmm. *So what would be the worst part of it do you think?*

Alisha: My dad moving out.

Me: *What would be so bad about that?*

Alisha: Mala and I wouldn't see him every day.

Me: Probably not. *How would you cope with not seeing him every day?*

Alisha: I wouldn't have a choice. I'd just have to get used to it I suppose . . . but I'm not sure I ever would.

Me: It might be really hard to get used to. But if that *did* happen – your dad moves out – *is there anything you could do to make it a bit better for you and Mala?*

Alisha: Just have to make the most of the times we did see him I suppose. Maybe he would get a place of his own like David's dad and we could stay over sometimes. We could still talk to him on the phone every night, I guess. We could make him cards. But you don't understand: it's not what I want. It just wouldn't be the same.

Me: You're absolutely right. It wouldn't be the same. It's the last thing you want to happen and maybe it won't. But the point is that if it did after a while *you would find ways to deal with it.*

Alisha: I was really sad when Grandma died and I thought that would never stop.

Me: *What helped you then?*

Alisha: Just talking to my mum about it.

Me: Do you think you would talk to your mum about how you would feel if your dad left? What about other people? Do you know anyone else whose dad doesn't live at home anymore?

Alisha: Oh yes. Loads of people in my class. Natalie's dad moved out last year and she seems okay now. But it's different when it's your own family.

Me: Yes it is. But the point is that your life would go on. And you would find ways to make it okay in the end because you are that kind of person too. Does it still seem so terrifying when you think about it now?

Alisha: Not as frightening exactly. Just really, really sad.

Teaching your child to look squarely at the very worst that could happen is, paradoxically, one of the techniques that children often find the most calming. Encouraging them to think beyond the point of crisis and consider what they could do to help themselves make the best of a bad situation reminds them that they are not completely powerless and brings anxiety levels down.

> Talk a child through something that worries them, using 'What if' and 'What then' to explore the worst-case scenario.

How likely is it?

Fear is very persuasive. It can make even the most unlikely scenarios seem like certainties. When frightened, most children do not even consider the other ways in which a given situation could work out because they remain fixated on the fearful outcome. In reality every event – good or bad – depends on a whole sequence of other events taking place first.

If I work as a doctor in a hospital you can safely assume

that I have been to medical school, that I have passed my medical board exams and that I have been successful in applying for a job there. These are all *necessary conditions* of my working there. Each anxiety scenario in your child's head also has a number of necessary conditions that have to be met, although when we are stressed or panicky we seldom stop to analyse them. Neither do we pause to think about the routes that would allow the meeting of these criteria or – more importantly – how likely each of these pathways is. In a child's head feared possibilities can easily become certainties. Teaching your child to dismantle and rate the likelihood of these scenarios can be a really helpful way to ground him.

Eleven-year-old Cassie had developed an obsessive anxiety that her father would be killed in a car crash on his way back from work. Every time she closed her eyes she pictured him bleeding to death in a heap of mangled wreckage at the side of the road. As a result she couldn't sleep until he returned to the house, which was often late at night.

Her mother helped Cassie to think systematically about the pieces that need to be in place in order to bring about the dreaded event. She realized that there were two necessary conditions without which the feared scenario was impossible: (1) her father had to be involved in a crash in the first place; and (2) he had to be so badly injured that the crash proved fatal.

Working together, Cassie and her mother came up with as many different pathways to fulfil the two necessary conditions as they could think of. Their list of factors potentially contributing to her father's involvement in an accident included:

- driving too fast
- falling asleep at the wheel
- being unable to avoid another out-of-control driver
- a tyre bursting or the car skidding on a wet patch
- daddy talking on the mobile and losing concentration.

By carefully exploring each of these possibilities in turn, Cassie was able to think more realistically about the likelihood of each one. She started monitoring how fast her father drove when she was in the car with him. Did he ever break the speed limit? What were her dad's views about people who did? Did she ever see him not wearing his seatbelt? By playing 'slaps' with her father Cassie established to her satisfaction that his reaction times were pretty quick, thereby reducing in her mind the likelihood that he would fail to respond swiftly if another car veered across the road.

Researching accurate factual information also helped Cassie rate the probability of the second necessary condition (her father being killed in the accident) more objectively. Using the Department of Transport data she discovered that, even if involved in a road accident, as a driver her father had less than a one in a hundred chance of being fatally injured.

By systematically breaking the feared scenario into its necessary conditions and then separately rating as a percentage the realistic probability of each contributing factor, Cassie found that the chances of completing *any* of the pathways she could imagine were much less than her fears were telling her. Moreover, since there were two necessary conditions in play, if each was independently quite unlikely, then the necessary combination of the two was even more improbable. In other words:

Unlikely event A × unlikely event B = **very** *unlikely* event C

As you will gather, the more necessary conditions that have to be met to bring about a particular disaster, the less chance it will happen (unless all the necessary conditions are highly likely to be met).

Even for much younger children, learning to look at the various components involved in the scenario they fear can be useful. If there are aspects of their anxieties that can be tested out then by all means set up your own mini-experiments. If there is factual information that your child can use to combat his fears then make sure he has access to it. All of these activities strengthen 'cool processing' capacities and can help them rein in an over-active imagination.

Self-soothing techniques

Simple self-soothing techniques are one of the most useful tools you can give your child. Most are easy and unobtrusive enough for your child to use in whatever settings she is in, and they really do work. In the case of babies and toddlers we instinctively provide our children with what they need to bring levels of agitation and distress back down. We hold them close to us, talk soothingly to them and use a rhythmic rocking or patting motion to restore their equilibrium. We may provide them with a distraction and give them something else to focus on. We do all these things instinctively and automatically. However, as our children grow older they are increasingly left to their own devices when it comes to dealing with escalating levels of internal stress.

Take a breather

Teaching your child to control his breathing takes only a few minutes, but studies show that deliberately practising the right kind of breathing is one of the easiest ways to reduce tension and induce a relaxed, calm state.

Different kinds of breathing are associated with different emotional states. When we are tense, frightened or anxious we tend to breathe in rapid, shallow breaths using our chest muscles to expand and contract our lungs. When we are relaxed our breathing is naturally smooth, deep and rhythmical. Relaxed breathing is co-ordinated by the muscles of the diaphragm – the wall between the chest and stomach cavity and it draws air deep into the lungs.

The fact is that it is very hard for the body to remain in a state of tension while diaphragmatic breathing is taking place. Diaphragmatic breathing is a powerful cue for the parasympathetic nervous system – the system designed to restore calm and tranquillity after the sympathetic nervous system has worked us up into a state of high arousal. Diaphragmatic breathing gives a message to your body to stand down from red alert. The mind–body connection means that as you calm yourself physically, so the mind automatically tends to settle too.

Whether your child is feeling stressed, panicky or angry, if she knows how to breathe properly she will be taking an important step towards restoring her equilibrium and short-circuiting the arousal that goes with emotional 'hot processing'.

> Deep breathing techniques can give your child an instant calming technique for times of distress.

To demonstrate this technique, get your child to place a hand on his stomach, just below his rib cage. Instruct him to focus on his hand and take a slow deep breath through his nose. Ask him to picture drawing air into his lungs so that they fill from the bottom. If he is doing this properly he should be able to feel his stomach pushing out slightly as the diaphragm depresses and there should only be a minimal rise and fall of his chest cavity.

Now encourage him to breathe in slowly to a count of five, hold the breath for a few seconds and then slowly exhale to another count of five. For children who struggle with this it can be helpful to get them to focus on the out breath rather than the inhalation. Ask your child to imagine that he has a lit candle a foot in front of him and that his job is to make the flame flicker just slightly for as long as he can without blowing it out until his lungs are empty. Remind him that when he needs to re-fill his lungs he should do so slowly through his nose. The sustained exhalation requires use of the diaphragm in a way that usually kicks off diaphragmatic breathing.

Once your child has mastered the art of diaphragmatic breathing you should also let him know that in order for it to have a reliable impact on his feelings he will need to do at least 3 sets of 10 breaths. Counting down from 10 to 1 while he does so also has a helpful, calming effect on most people. Next time you feel yourself getting worked up try diaphragmatic breathing for yourself. You will be impressed by the difference it makes.

Progressive muscle relaxation

This simple technique is based on the work of Edmund Jacobson, a doctor who discovered that by successively tensing and releasing different muscle groups throughout the body it was possible to induce a state of deep relaxation that really helped patients with conditions like high blood pressure, insomnia and colitis. Interestingly, later studies have established that *regular* practice of deep relaxation using this technique can increase people's sense of control over their emotions, as well as boosting self-esteem and improving all manner of anxiety symptoms.

Find a quiet place and a regular time for you and your child to practise this technique together. Before bed is an ideal time, especially since it is preferable not to use this technique on a full stomach. With younger children it can be good to do a shortened form of this very last thing when they are tucked up in bed and can hopefully drift off into a relaxed sleep.

1   Start off by getting your child to do a quick body scan and see whether she can detect any areas of particular tension. Tell her she doesn't have to change anything, just notice what she finds.

2   Then encourage your child to clench her fists as tight as possible and hold the pose for five to seven seconds. When she does let go encourage her to let her hands go completely limp. Throughout the state of tension and the state of release ask your child to concentrate on what she can feel in the relevant part of her body.

3   Move on to the biceps by getting your child to flex her forearms towards her shoulders as if lifting a heavy weight. Again get her to hold the position for a few seconds and then release. In between muscle groups spend about 20 seconds just focusing her

awareness on the steady rise and fall of her breathing.

4   The triceps can be can be tensed by extending the arms outwards and locking the elbows.

5   The forehead can be tensed by raising the eyebrows as high as possible.

6   Next get your child to screw her eyes shut as tight as she can and then relax.

7   Opening the jaw as wide as possible (the 'shark mouth'!) stretches the relevant muscles.

8   Next get your child to pull her head back into the floor or pillow as much as she can to tense and release the muscles around the neck. When she releases this pose encourage her to think of her head as something really heavy like a cannonball just resting there, trying to sink into the floor.

9   Hunch the shoulders up to the ears and release.

10 Ask your child next to see whether she can make her shoulder blades touch ... and let go.

11 Use a deep breath to expand the chest and hold it tense for a count of 5. Then release.

12 Then suck the stomach in as far as it will go. Let the tension flow away.

13 Arch the lower back.

14 Squeeze the buttocks together as tightly as possible – always guaranteed to produce a laugh ...

15 Clench the thighs.

16 Flex the feet to produce a stretch in the calf muscles. Again let the pose go.

17 Ask your child to curl up her toes as much as she can.

18 Finally, get her to repeat the body scan and check that nothing is still tight or tense. Instruct her to follow the gentle rise and fall of her breathing and enjoy the sensations of comfort and relaxation.

As anxiety expert Edmund Bourne points out, to enjoy the maximum benefits, this routine should ideally be practised for about twenty minutes a day. Now I am well aware this is not a realistic proposition for many busy parents. However, even if you use an abbreviated version of this technique, perhaps just concentrating on one or two muscle groups, you are still laying the foundation of a useful skill. You could also consider making your child a personalized relaxation tape so he can practise on his own.

> Learning to tense and release different muscles is relaxing for both body and mind.

If your child is in a situation in which he needs to calm down, just getting him to clench hands and forearms as tight as he can for a few seconds before letting go provides a simple physical ritual for discharging excess stress. Like the diaphragmatic breathing, even a partial experience of muscle relaxation can coax body and mind into a more composed state.

Just imagine . . . The calming power of visualization

The last two methods of self-soothing have involved changing a physical state to affect a mental one. With visualization the direction is reversed: the resources of the mind are used to dampen down the body's stress reaction. The mind is very powerful and the power of suggestion alone has enabled people to sit through painful dental treatment without analgesia. The robustness of the placebo effect – the fact that simply believing you are taking a helpful drug works in many cases as well as taking an actual drug – testifies to how a state of mind can influence our experience and even alter our physical state.

If your child becomes sufficiently practised at using creative visualization techniques she will be able to use this technique to calm herself down. However, as with all these techniques, I would emphasize that the more your child practises them, the more effective they will be when she needs to rely on them.

Visualization alone is sufficiently powerful to put most people into a relaxed state. If most people spend five minutes picturing themselves lying on a beautiful, sunlit beach their heart rate drops, their respiration rate changes and the level of electrical resistance that can be measured by skin sensors increases. Their brains also start generating more alpha waves, a pattern of activity associated with meditation, day-dreaming and deep relaxation.

A safe place

'Whenever things get difficult at school or Jody is mean to me,' said Alice, looking earnestly at me through her deep green eyes, 'I just go to my Gran's house and I always feel better.' 'That's great', I said, thinking to myself how helpful it was that Alice evidently had such a close, supportive relationship with her grandmother. However, when I later reported this back her mother looked a bit perplexed. 'Alice did have a really close bond with my mother ... ,' she told me, 'but the thing is she died four years ago.' Only then did I realize that Alice had spontaneously come up with a solution often taught to children who are having difficulty managing their feelings: she had created a mental refuge into which she could retreat whenever toxic emotions like anxiety or fear threatened to take control.

Why not help your child to create an imaginary sanctuary of his own? He may want to base this on a particularly pleasant memory, a time in his life when he felt especially secure and happy. Try and avoid memories of anywhere too active or stimulating. However good a time you all had on Space Mountain at Disneyland it probably isn't the ideal focus for this kind of meditation. If your child is having difficulty thinking of a real time and place, feel free to encourage him to create one. It just has to be somewhere that feels safe and relaxing. Children I have known have chosen locations ranging from caves to jungles, although a tropical beach is always a good default option.

> Encourage your child to visualize herself in a relaxing setting – and ideally create a personal 'safe place' she can think about when the need arises.

The two keys to making the safe place visualization work for your child are: (1) linking it to a state of physical relaxation – perhaps using the breathing exercises or progressive muscle relaxation techniques just reviewed; and (2) making the scene as vivid as possible. Ideally your child needs to flesh out the detail using all five senses. What colours and textures can he see? What does the sand feel like under foot? What is the temperature like? Is there a breeze blowing over his skin or is everything perfectly still? Can he smell the pine needles in the forest?

As he develops the scene, deliberately draw your child's attention to how he feels within it. Use words like 'relaxed', 'calm' and 'peaceful' in the description. Get your child to notice how his body feels when he thinks about this scene – how comfortable it feels to be there, how heavy and slack his limbs have become. Get him to tune into the steady rhythm of his heartbeat and the gentle rise and fall of his breathing.

After a few minutes ask him to come up with a single word that summarizes the scene and what he is feeling. Ask him to touch together the thumb and forefinger of his right hand while he repeats that word silently in his mind.

If your child practises this for five minutes a day, before long the simple act of bringing his thumb and finger together and saying his anchor word will be sufficient to conjure up the sense of relaxation associated with the safe place. He can then use this to counteract waves of panic, anger, acute stress or general anxiety when they occur. The really good news is that studies suggest the generalization effects of a regular relaxation practice mean that he is also less likely to experience these emotions in such an intense form.

For many children the knowledge that there is something they can do to bring themselves back into a more collected state is a great comfort. Once they have overcome the initial hurdle of practising sufficiently for the image to produce a reliable effect, even very young children say that it makes a real difference and many like to think about their safe place just before they go to sleep.

More visualization ideas to combat anxiety

In Chapter 3 we looked at how beneficial it can be for a child to personify the source of negative emotions in his life and invent a magical solution to disarm it. Visualization techniques can also be enlisted to replace one emotion with another. The following are just a few suggestions for images that children can use. Feel free to invent your own together.

The hourglass Get your child to picture his anxious feelings as bright red sand in an old-fashioned hourglass (you may have to get hold of one if your child doesn't know what this is). Explain that however hard he might try the grains of sand cannot stay in the upper chamber. Encourage your child to imagine his anxiety slowly through the neck of the hourglass under gravity's influence until the top chamber is completely empty. Repeat this process until your child feels calmer. A similar image to explore is bathwater swirling down the plughole. Don't rush this one: picturing the slow trickle of the sand or water over a sustained period gives the parasympathetic nervous system time to do its work.

Lighten up ... For this visualization ask your child to imagine unwanted stressful feelings as a sickly, pulsing colour radiating outwards from wherever the anxiety is felt most strongly in her body. This will usually be the solar plexus or the head. Make sure your child has a clear mental image of this before you move on to the next stage.

As your child breathes in using the diaphragmatic breathing described above, ask her to imagine she is drawing cool, pure light into her body from a point at the top of her head. As she breathes, help her picture the cleansing light becoming steadily stronger and brighter, working its way through the cells of her whole body.

As her body fills with light, ask her what is happening to the anxious coloured mist she began with. Some children will naturally picture the light neutralizing the mist as it grows more intense. Others will talk about the white light 'pushing the mist out'. Work with whatever your child suggests, but emphasize that the two cannot occupy the same space, and that the white light is much more powerful. Keep going until your child can imagine her whole body pulsating with the white light and all traces of the anxiety mist have been dispelled. As with the hourglass, you may need to repeat this exercise several times before the desired result is achieved.

> Use guided visualization techniques to help your child get rid of anxious feelings by imagining them draining away – or being pushed out by something stronger and more positive.

Mental dress rehearsals If your child is anxious about a specific future event it can be helpful to use visualization in much the same way as sports psychologists encourage athletes to do before they run a race. Mentally rehearsing each step of the event in detail and picturing a positive outcome can shift children into a more optimistic mindset. It will also help them activate the inner resources that make the desired outcome more likely. If they are struggling to do this, the point at which their mental projection becomes derailed can often help identify the crux of the problem. Knowing this, you and your child can then use the problem-solving strategies discussed in Chapter 7 to come up with solutions to any specific difficulties.

Lifestyle issues

Physically active children tend to be less stressed as a rule than passive ones. Exercise can play a valuable role in building children's resistance to stress and all the figures are suggesting that our children play less sport and spend more time in front of various screens than ever before. Only 1 in 10 children currently achieves the 90 minutes a day of physical activity currently recommended by the government. Find out what physical activities your child enjoys and create opportunities for him to pursue them. Do physically demanding things together and make such activities part of your family life.

Yoga is a particularly good way of teaching children to relax, as well as having several other health benefits. There are many good children's yoga classes dotted around the country and they can be particularly helpful for children who find it hard to be still and quiet. So just because you cannot imagine your child fitting into such a class don't rule it out. The fact that they are surrounded by other engaged children, combined with the fact they will have to concentrate in order to hold some of the positions successfully can have a transformative effect. Again, if you have an established yoga or meditation practice of your own, your child is likely to be much more receptive to the idea of joining in.

The role that diet may play in relation to childhood stress has yet to be conclusively resolved. However, nutrition experts such as Alexander Schauss believe that a diet that is excessively rich in unrefined carbohydrates requires more B vitamins than the body often has available, with the result that such vitamins are 'borrowed' from the nervous system. This, he argues, can increase susceptibility to stress and lead to all manner of behavioural problems. There is also some evidence that removing junk food from the diets of children with Attention Deficit Hyperactivity Disorder (ADHD) can help some children, although results from these studies are not consistent.

What is clear is that if children eat a lot of sugary foods they can end up trapped into a boom–bust cycle of 'sugar rushes'. These are hard for the body to cope with and can also lead to manic, out-of-control behaviour. Although we have yet to fully understand the relationship between diet and the nervous system, suffice it to say that a healthy, balanced diet is more likely to provide the brain with the nutrients it needs to function well.

Finally, do make sure your child is getting enough sleep. It is no coincidence that sleep deprivation is one of the methods used to stress torture victims. A school-age child needs 10 hours sleep on average and pre-schoolers more than this. Be aware that, due to a perversity of the adolescent body clock, teenagers are naturally inclined to go to bed later and wake later in the morning – a fact not accommodated by the schedule of the school day. This means that your adolescent children may have to train themselves to rest at times when their body clock is telling them otherwise. Good sleeping habits are a discipline that has to be learned. Many parents these days let children dictate their own bed times and this is a big mistake. Children often think they need less sleep than they do, and a tired child is much more vulnerable to stress and much more likely to be crotchety and short-tempered.

Don't leave it to chance

In order to sustain 'good behaviour', a child must subdue all kinds of urges and instincts. This is hard work that makes real demands on his mental resources. Stress has been defined as the state that occurs 'when a situation exceeds our available resources to cope' so if your child is already stressed he is going to find it extremely difficult to deal with any additional demands that are made of him. In practice this means that a stressed or anxious child is inevitably much more likely to be a badly behaved one.

In view of this, keeping an eye on your child's stress levels and giving him practical strategies to manage stress is essential if you don't want to end up in the company of a child who can no longer regulate his own conduct – a sure-fire recipe for putting your own stress levels up!

You cannot shield your child from the stresses of life, but you can give her skills to disarm and diffuse their effects. You wouldn't send a soldier into battle without adequate protection, but that is precisely what we often do to children when we send them into the world without knowing how to handle stress and anxiety properly. Some people work out ways to help themselves, but the process of trial and error can be a long and costly business. It is far better that you equip your children with stress management tools while they still have their lives ahead of them than wait for a nervous breakdown, relationship failure or a heart attack to provide an unwelcome wake-up call in adulthood. Being stressed and anxious is a miserable experience. As a parent you have an opportunity to make a real difference to your child's quality of life (and your own) by taking the time to teach these basic skills. It is well worth it.

 ## Quick summary action points

- Learn to recognize the signs of a child under stress.

- Be careful what you let your children watch on TV – they can worry about things more than you might think.

- Be conscious of potential pressures at school. Don't place an unhealthy emphasis on achievement.

- Tread carefully around your child's 'symbols of self' and be sensitive to underlying insecurities.

- Recognize that children often find change stressful and prepare your child if a change is on the horizon.

- Too much stimulation can be stressful – and so can too little. Help your child understand what he needs and help him to achieve the right balance.

- Consider using graded exposure to help your child face her fears.

- Diffuse anxiety by getting your child to look squarely at the worst-case scenario rather than avoiding it.

- Help your child calculate the likelihood of the things he fears.

- Help your child master self-soothing techniques like diaphragmatic breathing, progressive muscle relaxation and visualization.

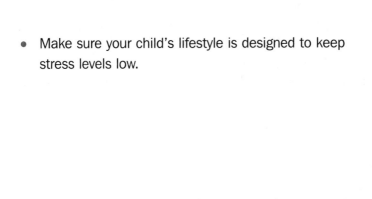

- Make sure your child's lifestyle is designed to keep stress levels low.

6
People powers

Cultivating social confidence

Whether or not you agree with the philosopher Jean-Paul Sartre that 'Hell is other people', if children are unable to relate well to others this can make life very difficult for them and those around them. Human beings are supremely social animals and we live our whole lives entangled with the lives of others. 'Bad behaviour' often occurs when children's ability to relate appropriately breaks down. This means that equipping children with tools to negotiate the complex world of human relationships has to be a priority for any parent who wants their child to cope with the strong emotions other people can trigger. Being able to engage successfully with others and control your reactions to them is a prerequisite of a fulfilled, happy life.

In this chapter we will look at how you can help your children stay in control when provoked, and how you can coach them in the principles of clear and assertive communication so they can handle other children more confidently. We will also take a brief look at the dynamics of groups, and think about how you can help your child to feel they belong without getting caught up in the more destructive undercurrents of group life.

We'll start by focusing on the management of an emotion that can wreak havoc with your child's relationships and behaviour both inside and outside the family. Children are particularly vulnerable to it but, if left unchecked, this emotion can also establish habits that will do real damage to their adult lives as well. This emotion is anger.

The up-side of anger

Because of its destructive power, anger has received a very bad press. It is true that the anger of children is responsible for some of the most mortifying moments of parenthood: an enraged child is capable of saying and doing just about anything. Nevertheless, what your children need to understand is that anger is a perfectly normal emotion that we all experience, and that it is only *uncontrolled* anger that leads to such undesirable consequences. So we can understand the more positive face of anger, let's briefly consider the circumstances under which children tend to see red.

Children usually get angry in three situations. Firstly, when they feel under attack – either physically or verbally – anger galvanizes them to strike back. Just as the puffer fish instantly inflates itself to several times its resting size when threatened, angry behaviour warns potential predators to back off. The difficulty is that the limbic system of the brain which drives the anger response does not pause to calibrate the true extent of the threat, so the reaction can be completely out of proportion to the original cause.

Secondly, children often become angry and frustrated when they are blocked from achieving their goals. This is why it so often difficult for children to play together. Successful collaboration inevitably involves a trade-off between your own needs and those of the people you are playing with. Keeping control under such circumstances is very difficult for some children – as a million overturned board games can testify. This is also why practising self-control within the context of play is so valuable.

Thirdly, children are easily angered by situations in which they feel their rights are being violated. The universal childhood protest of 'It's not fair!' often heralds an angry outburst. Children are wedded to principles like fairness, honesty and responsibility (in other people at least) not least because they depend upon such values to police the way other people treat them. In situations where these principles are not enforced children know they are vulnerable.

In each case anger is serving a valid self-protective function. Anger is designed to protect us against the encroachments of other people, to maintain our sense of personal power and hold others to account if they overstep the mark. In themselves these are all worthy aims, but your child needs to understand that if his anger is not to backfire and cause more problems than it solves it needs to be appropriate to the circumstance and, more importantly, harnessed in a controlled fashion.

Race against the clock

Children who struggle with anger need to know that they have only a few seconds in which to act if they are to stand any chance of retaining self-control. For many there will swiftly be a point of no return beyond which all chance of self-restraint is lost.

For this reason it is essential that your child becomes very familiar with the tell-tale signs of an impending explosion. These symptoms vary between individuals, so when the dust settles after your child's next eruption sit down and help him identify the changes that let him know he is about to flare up. The warning signs can be physical, emotional or cognitive. Overleaf is a list of some of the symptoms children report, but be aware that your own child may be conscious of others or conceive them in his own unique style.

- 'My heart beats really fast'
- Feeling of tightness in the chest
- 'I can't get my breath properly'
- Butterflies in the stomach
- Muscle tension
- 'It's like this ball in my tummy gets heavier and heavier'
- Sensation of pressure around the head
- Feeling wound up inside
- Increased agitation: 'I start to get really fidgety'
- 'The other person's face gets really big ... like in a close-up'
- Fists clenching
- Sensation of 'building pressure'
- Feeling slightly sick
- Prickly heat on the back of neck
- 'I hear bad words ... swears in my head'
- Problems thinking straight
- Sensation of things closing down – tunnel vision
- Red-mist descending
- 'I get this roaring sound in my ears'
- 'I picture myself hurting the other person really badly'
- 'Remembering other times when I got really angry'

- Wave of sudden, unnatural stillness: the calm before the storm

- 'My feelings switch off just before it takes over'

Explain to your child that the nature of anger means he cannot afford to hang around. The minute he starts to notice any of his personal warning signs he needs to act decisively and quickly using the traffic light rule.

The traffic light rule

The presence of any of these anger symptoms is an automatic red light. The moment she detects them your child needs to **STOP** what she is doing *immediately* and remove herself from the situation so she can regain control. Anger is often linked to particular setting, and physically removing yourself from that place is one of the most effective steps you can take to reduce its intensity.

If your child is in a situation where it is impossible to leave she can achieve some sense of distance by imagining herself viewing the scene (still with her in it) as if she is looking down from a corner of the ceiling. Shifting perspective like this, and viewing the situation from the outside, creates detachment and engages cool processing mechanisms that automatically make the nervous system less reactive. Reassure your child that getting out is not the same as opting out. She can still address the problem that led to the mounting anger once she has regained control. In fact, it is important that she does so. More about this shortly.

> Train your children to spot their anger warning signs – and to stop whatever they are doing immediately when the signs appear, ideally by leaving the room or situation.

The orange light phase is the one that your child uses to restore her equilibrium. Diaphragmatic breathing and safe place visualization are invaluable during this stage (see page 145) but the key thing is to delay response, maybe using a tactic as simple as counting down slowly from 20.

An image that children of all ages find useful is to think of their anger as a leaking bucket with holes in the bottom. Stressful situations can pour in water so fast that unless we are careful the bucket overflows. However, if we can stop adding to the bucket and just wait, even if we do nothing else, the water that is already there will trickle out. Anger tells our brains that we need to follow through straight away. If we exercise self-control and do nothing, our lack of response will eventually mean that our emotions fall into line with what our body is doing (or in this case *not* doing).

For children who have trouble calming themselves, one trick they could try is sucking a boiled sweet. The reason this works is that the sucking reflex is associated with states of calm and comfort in newborn children. Also, the brain cannot experience states of pleasure and fury at the same time, so if your child is enjoying the flavour of something in his mouth it will be more difficult for him to remain quite as worked up.

> Use tactics to help release anger – such as sucking a sweet, or counting slowly, or simply waiting and doing nothing until the anger subsides.

The orange light phase also gives your child the chance to review the situation and ask himself the following crucial questions:

- Why am I angry?
- How angry do I feel? (score this from 1 to 10)
- How angry *should* I feel in this situation, out of 10?
- What will happen to *me* if I give in to my anger right now?
- Can I think of a way of getting what I need which doesn't involve me losing control?

Only when anger levels have dropped to a maximum of 2 or 3 out of 10 should your child give herself a green light to return to the original situation. Once your child is back in control, this is the stage at which she needs to use assertive communication. At the very least she needs to tell the person concerned how she felt and, if possible, negotiate a solution to the original conflict. Children who manage to diffuse their anger in the short term but don't find constructive ways to address the forces driving it often end up turning their rage inwards and can become stressed and depressed.

> Help your children address the cause of the anger when they are calm – even if it's only telling the person who triggered it that they felt angry and why.

Are they *really* out to get you?

If anger is a protective response, it stands to reason that angry people feel threatened a lot of the time. The way they think is one way angry children keep this sense of threat turned to maximum. If your child is prone to anger, he may need to train himself out of habits of thought that turn even the most innocent of situations into something more ominous.

'He was *deliberately* trying to wind me up by singing that song over and over again so I had to hit him to make him stop . . .' Hardly audible over the howls of his younger brother, this explanation was offered to me by my elder son who clearly believed that, under such circumstances, punching his brother was an entirely reasonable response.

My son was displaying one of the most common thought habits of angry people: he had ascribed a malevolent motive almost guaranteed to trigger an aggressive response. Now his brother loves to sing and does have a tendency to latch onto a particular phrase and repeat it *ad nauseam*, sometimes to the accompaniment of an exotic dance move of his own devising. After a while (and I hope he will forgive me for saying so in a public forum) this can be pretty irritating. However, my eldest son leapt almost instantly from irritation to full-scale physical aggression because he convinced himself that my youngest son had *intentionally* set out to annoy him. In his mind that was the only possible meaning of his younger brother's action.

Admittedly, this might actually have been the case. However, the point is my elder son was not in a mood to consider alternative explanations. Consequently he neither pointed out the effect the song was having on him, nor asked his brother to go and sing it elsewhere. Assuming it was intended to be a personal affront he let his fists do the talking and got sent to bed early as a result.

This kind of mind-reading act is typical of the way angry people of all ages read other people's intentions. It is really important to encourage children to question their assumptions about other people's motives if you don't want them to be ruled by anger. Teach them to look for innocent explanations and extenuating circumstances.

Emotive language

In a similar vein, help your child listen out for the way he describes situations to himself. Angry people tend to see things in terms of extremes, and their language often reflects this. 'It just shows that Charlie and Hakeem *hate* me and I can't stand them. They're *so* selfish. They're my very worst enemies,' complained Fergus, aged 6, about two of his classmates. When his father probed a bit further it turned out that almost everything Fergus had just told him was blatantly untrue.

There was no evidence that Charlie and Hakeem 'hated' Fergus and the many hours the three boys had happily played together suggested it wasn't the case that Fergus couldn't 'stand' them either. Charlie and Hakeem had not even been especially 'selfish' – they had just declined to swap a star player football card for the lower value cards Fergus was offering. However, once Fergus had translated the situation into such powerfully emotive terms he was halfway to convincing himself these boys were his sworn enemies. Always watch out for language in your child's speech that accentuates a sense of threat, animosity or rivalry and teach him to be on guard against it.

> Help your child to see that irritating or hurtful events were not necessarily *designed* to irritate or hurt.

Maintaining the angry person's position that the world is a dangerous place full of people who want to harm or take advantage of you requires the opposite of rose-tinted glasses. Angry children focus in on the evidence that supports their beliefs – and ignore facts that don't fit. Help your child to use the sort of courtroom skills described in Chapter 3 to achieve a more objective evaluation of the situation.

Taking a stand

Beth was one of the shyest 10 year olds I have met. When she came into the room she stared at the ground and said nothing at all for the first 20 minutes. I tried without success to ask her a few gentle questions. When I got no response I started to speculate about what she might be feeling. I asked her to nod if I was on the right track. I continued in a similar vein until it occurred to me that Beth was simply agreeing with *everything* put to her. If I had suggested she had six heads and worked down a mine she probably wouldn't have contradicted me. It came as no great surprise to learn that Beth was being bullied at school. One thing was clear: whatever else was required, she needed to become much more assertive.

What is assertive communication?

Assertiveness is a set of skills that help us to stand up for ourselves without feeling overly anxious. They enable us to express ourselves clearly and defend our rights, while also behaving respectfully towards other people. Assertive communication involves a few basic principles that can be mastered by even young children, but many children are never taught them.

Ironically, the children who benefit most from assertiveness training are those usually considered to be the most forceful in their dealings with others. Angry, aggressive children often act in this way because they lack confidence in their ability to get their needs met by any other means. They often fail to speak up before it is too late, stockpiling festering resentments that could have been diffused if the individual had been able to express her feelings clearly at the time.

It is crucial to teach your child the difference between being assertive and being aggressive. Many children find it hard to grasp the distinction. One of the most straightforward ways to do this is to think about the differences between the ways in which angry, confident and shy people behave. Set your child the task of observing the people he meets, as well as thinking about characters in TV dramas, books or comics. Ask him to think about the way people in these three categories use their bodies, as well as what they say and how they speak. Beth's list read as follows:

Aggressive/ angry	Confident	Shy
• Shouty	• Relaxed	• Looks at floor
• Swears at people	• Looks you in the eye	• Hunches over
• Comes up too close	• Speaks clearly	• Doesn't speak much
• Wags finger and points a lot	• Stands tall	• Apologises even when things not her fault
• Fierce expression	• Doesn't react	• Hesitates
• Threatening	• Means what he says	• Doesn't look at you
• Blows up easily	• Strong, not pushed around	• Weak voice
• Unpopular	• Stays calm	• Feels panicky
• Rude	• Shows feelings	• Follows lead of other people
• Looks out of control	• Can say 'no' and disagree	

Sounding like you mean it

Once she had achieved a clearer idea about what she was aiming for, Beth had to work on the way she talked to people. She was asked to apply three simple principles:

1 Practise using 'I' statements as much as possible.

2 Keep it concise.

3 Say it loud and clear.

The use of 'I' statements is usually a hallmark of assertive people. Nervous people lack the confidence to take ownership of their wishes and opinions, whereas aggression speaks a language of blame that focuses on the perceived failings of the other person: 'You always put me down . . .', 'Why can't you be more understanding?', 'You're such a jerk!'

For children like Beth, learning to use phrases such as 'I think . . .', 'I feel . . .', 'I want . . .', can feel very exposing to begin with. Ironically for such a bashful girl, Beth believed that if she used the first person like this people would see her as selfish and egotistical. However, Beth soon found it empowering to communicate her views and feelings in a more direct, transparent way.

Beth also recognized that her tentative, rambling way of talking when she did speak was giving people the impression that they didn't have to take her seriously. She set herself the challenge of trying to use as few words as possible when asking for things, even though she was worried this would sound rude. Rewarding her for dropping specific speech mannerisms like clearing her throat before she spoke and using hesitation phenomena (excessive use of 'um . . .' and 'er . . .') also helped make her sound more focused and confident.

Beth also had a tendency to let her voice drift away at the end of sentences and allow the pitch to get higher, giving her speech a slightly whining, wheedling quality that made her sound weak. She corrected this by imagining the final word of her sentences as the bull's-eye towards which she was aiming a vocal 'arrow'. She learned to target the end of the sentence with sufficient force to prevent her delivery drifting off course and kept her tone more level. To stop her being so softly spoken she was encouraged to visit a nearby motorway bridge and compete with the volume of the traffic.

> Discuss the differences between aggressive, assertive and shy behaviour with your child and help him work out how to shift his behaviour in the direction needed.

Looking like you mean it

It was not just Beth's verbal communication skills that were letting her down. Her stooped posture and avoidance of eye contact was also giving an unhelpful message. Rather than adopting the posture of the 'hibernating hedgehog', she was encouraged to 'face the gale'. This involved standing as if a strong wind was blowing against her, planting her feet squarely on the deck, pulling her shoulders back, and holding her head up. Beth learned that although her averted gaze made her appear submissive, too much eye contact could be misinterpreted as threatening. She got used to holding the other person's gaze for a couple of seconds, glancing away momentarily, and then looking back. When she was making a strong 'I' statement Beth was reminded to make sure that she always ended her sentence looking directly at the other person.

A winning formula

Although by changing the way she presented herself Beth was starting to create a very different impression, the real test was whether she could use her new skills to deal with the constant teasing she faced at school. Previously when this occurred Beth would typically say nothing and beat a hasty retreat. She needed to try something new. It was agreed that the next time one of the girls at school was unpleasant to her she would use the following protocol:

1 Give a brief, factual description of the situation as you see it.

2 Let the other person know what you feel in this situation using the formula: 'When you do X, I feel Y.'

3 Make a strong statement of your own desire or need.

4 Give a clear warning about the action you will take if that need is not met.

When Beth arrived at her next session I could tell she was pleased with herself. Apparently the ringleader of the girls bullying her had made some snide remark about her appearance in the corridor as she passed by. Rather than pretending she had not heard, Beth had confronted the girl and dealt assertively with the situation:

> 'I heard what you said about my clothes just now [step 1]. When you make those kind of comments I feel upset and angry [step 2]. I want you to stop making fun of me [step 3]. If you don't stop I am going straight to Miss Jenkins because I have had enough of all this [step 4].'

Impressively, she had not even waited for a reply but turned smartly on her heels and walked briskly away. Beth could hear the other girls giggling in embarrassment behind her, but reported that they had steered clear of her for the rest of that week. 'To be honest,' she said, 'I don't really care if they carry on. I shouldn't care what people like that think about me anyway.' Acting more assertively was affecting not only how Beth was perceived by others, but also how she was feeling about herself.

Know your rights

One of the reasons that children often fail to stick up for themselves is simply because they are not clear about what they are entitled to expect from other people. It is worth helping school-age children compose a personal 'Bill of Rights' so they can achieve some sense of clarity about this issue. Children need to decide what they are entitled to, what standards to maintain, and where the line falls between acceptable and unacceptable behaviour.

We noted earlier that respect is a key component of assertiveness, but truly assertive behaviour is not just about encouraging respectful behaviour from others, but also demonstrating respect in your dealings with them. One of the benefits of taking the time to think about a personal bill of rights is that it also provides children with clear guidelines as to how they can conduct themselves in ways that respect other people's rights too.

When your child has come up with 5–10 principles that he is happy with, take the time to word-process or write them out neatly. Perhaps you could even frame the document and put it up somewhere where he will see it every day. Encourage your child to approach this task in his own way, but if the bill is to function as a useful benchmark for assertive behaviour it should probably include some of the following principles:

I have a right ...

- To say what I think
- To express my feelings and wishes
- To be treated with respect
- To live my life without being bullied or manipulated
- To be myself
- To stick up for my rights
- To respect the rights of others
- To use my talents and abilities
- To choose how I respond to other people

Do keep in mind that the process of becoming more assertive and finding the delicate bite point between confidence and aggression is one that children can take a while to perfect. Sometimes the situations they encounter in the playground can challenge even the most assertive individual. Be on hand to provide extra support and coaching when needed.

Most children learn best by doing, so if you are attempting to help your child develop a more assertive demeanour it is important to give her opportunities to practise the skills as much as possible. Prepare your child for encounters with aggressive or critical people by role-playing conflict situations beforehand. In the heat of the moment it can be hard for children to remember what they should do, but if they are well-rehearsed the appropriate responses should come much more readily to hand.

> Use current real-life situations to 'rehearse' the best things to say to handle situations assertively.

When your child does have to hold his ground the following techniques can also be useful.

The broken record

Let your child know that one of the keys to assertiveness is persistence. He needs to be able to deflect attempts to push him off course or de-rail his efforts to get his needs met. One of the simplest ways of doing this is to employ a technique referred to as 'the broken record'. This simply involves calmly restating your position until the other person is forced to acknowledge it. It works most powerfully if the need can be expressed in a single, concise statement that can be repeated as many times as necessary – hence the term 'broken record'. Rather than engaging with the other person's arguments or distraction techniques, someone using this technique simply restates his main point until his opponent gives up.

In the example below Danny uses the broken record technique to resist the pressure applied by his friend Steve to let him copy his homework.

Steve: Come on Danny ... Help me out here ... At least let me copy the last few questions. Mr Wilson's going to kill me if I don't hand anything in this week. I'll owe you ...

Danny: I'm really sorry Steve. You're a good mate and I don't want you to get into trouble but it doesn't feel right. *I just don't feel comfortable letting you copy my work.*

Steve: What's the harm in it? It's not going to cost you anything: you've done it already.

Danny: That's not the point. It took me ages. Besides which, if you copy the answers you're still not going to understand any of it.

Steve: So are you saying I'm thick now?

Danny: No, I am not. *I just don't feel comfortable letting you copy my work.*

Steve: You can be a real jerk sometimes. I've done loads of stuff for you. What about when I stood up for you against that Year 8 kid? Or lent you my Nintendo for all those weeks when you were sick?

Danny: I really appreciate those things, Steve, but this is different. *I just don't feel comfortable letting you copy.*

Steve: Maybe what you're really worried about is other people getting as good marks as you. Is that it? Poor little Danny worried he's not going to be top of the class? Not going to be King of the Swots any more?

Danny: Steve, you can try and wind me up all you want. *I don't feel comfortable about letting you copy.* It's not going to happen. Look, I can't help you this time, but if you want we can study together next week.

Steve: I thought you were supposed to be my friend . . .

Danny: I am your friend but –

Steve: [mimicking Danny] '*I don't feel comfortable about letting you copy my work . . .*' I get it alright? God, you're such a loser. [Steve storms off]

Anyone using this technique, whether adult or child, should be aware that it can prove highly frustrating for the other person. By refusing to be drawn in, Danny leaves Steve effectively beating his head against a brick wall. The broken record is a form of passive resistance and, although often effective, it can create considerable resentment. Normally, assertive communication always attempts to find a compromise that protects the self-esteem of both parties but, as in this example, this is not always possible.

> Explain that sometimes people will try to argue instead of accepting how you feel, and how to hold your ground when this happens.

Fogging

In the martial art of Aikido the student is taught that the most effective way to counter an attack is not to meet it head-on but to 'blend' with the motion of the attacker. In doing so you turn your opponent's strength against her. Fogging relies upon a similar principle. The key is to search for something in your adversary's remarks that you can agree upon – at least in principle. Most arguments involve disagreement and the defence of a fixed position by both parties. By fogging your child aims to disarm his opponent by working to establish some common ground. Because this technique requires some sophistication and the ability to think quickly on your feet, it is usually more appropriate for older children.

In the following example teenager Dinah employs a fogging technique to tackle a stream of put-downs from her brother Marcus.

Marcus: I can't believe you're on the computer again. Don't you ever do anything else but Facebook these days?

Dinah: You're right, my sweet little brother. I have been spending a lot of time at the computer recently. [*fogging*]

Marcus: Has it ever occurred to you that other people might want to go on it sometimes?

Dinah: Perhaps I am being a bit selfish. [*fogging*]

Marcus: I am surprised you and your loser friends have got that much to say to each other.

Dinah: I can see that you might be surprised by that. [*fogging*]

Marcus: You're probably spending all your time talking about boyfriends. I don't know why: with a face like that you're never going to get one!

Dinah: Mmmm. I can see that the way you feel about me might make it hard for you to imagine that anyone else might find me attractive. [*fogging*]

Marcus: You could at least make more of an effort with yourself.

Dinah: [smiles sweetly] You're absolutely right Marcus. I probably could pay more attention to my appearance. [*fogging*]

Marcus: You're weirding me out, sis. What's wrong with you today?

Dinah: You have a point, Marcus. I certainly don't seem to be reacting to you like I usually do. [*fogging*] I appreciate that may be making you feel uncomfortable. [*fogging*]

Marcus: Mum! Dinah's freaking me out. Make her stop!

Fogging can be a very effective way of dealing with verbal bullying. When bullies use insults they are trying to provoke a reaction. Although the content of a fogging response may look submissive insofar as the attack is not actively resisted, if the person using the technique can retain an aura of unperturbed calm it can be very powerful.

In some cases pushing agreement to a point at which it becomes ludicrous or comical can completely take the wind out of an aggressor's sails. One 9-year-old boy responded to a bully's taunt of 'You're a girl ... you're a girl' after missing a penalty by responding: 'Yes. You're absolutely right. I am completely female. Just look at my long flowing hair and girlish clothes. I am the biggest girl ever and now I need to leave because I am late for a netball match. Do you want a kiss?' Everyone around fell about laughing and the insult completely backfired.

Learning to negotiate

On a daily basis your child will encounter situations in which his own wishes and needs are going to clash with those of other people. Learning how to handle these situations is a critical life skill that children need to start practising as soon as possible. Try and reinforce the following principles whenever you have the opportunity:

- Help your child to understand that life isn't a competition. It's not just about getting what you want, but about finding solutions where everybody gets some of what they want. If two people have both given a bit of ground but leave happy, that's a much bigger success than getting your way but leaving another person feeling squashed.

- Emphasize that for negotiations to work it is essential

to maintain a respectful and considerate attitude towards the other person. If people feel attacked they will be in no mood to compromise.

- Remind your child that one way to do this is by openly and directly acknowledging the other person's feelings, needs and concerns: 'It's horrid to feel left out...', 'Let's find a way to do it that's fair for everyone...'

- Successful negotiation depends as much on listening as it does on talking. Encourage your child to ask questions that help her fully understand the other person's point of view.

- Stress the importance of keeping an open mind. Help your child to think flexibly and creatively in the search for solutions. Children can be very blinkered at times and assume that there is only one answer to a given problem. This is seldom the case.

- Reinforce the importance of keeping a cool head. If things are getting heated, teach your child that the best way forward may be to take a break for a few minutes and return to the negotiating table once everyone has calmed down.

The foundation of these skills can be laid with even very young children using games that teach the value of collaboration or compromise to achieve their goals. Comprehension and memory games in which competitors have to answer questions about narrated stories in return for sweets or other token rewards can also train young infants to listen attentively. Simple piece-collecting games like 'Go fish' or 'Beetle' can be modified so that players can exchange missing pieces and have to bargain and compromise accordingly. Older children can learn much about negotiation principles from games like 'Monopoly'. The wheeling and dealing involved can nurture skilled negotiators – as well as providing useful lessons as to how and why negotiations can so easily break down.

> From an early age, games can be used to teach listening skills, negotiation, collaboration and compromise.

Understanding groups

Children's participation in groups moulds their experience in profound ways. The chances are that the real highs and lows of your child's experience will be determined by what happens in groups – whether friendship groups, school classes or the family. The importance of different groups waxes and wanes over the course of a child's development but psychologist Judith Harris claims that, even pre-adolescence, the influence of peers may rival that of parents. Because children cannot avoid groups, and because of the significant role they will play in their lives, it makes sense for you and your child to understand something about the ways groups operate.

More than meets the eye

Psychologists who have studied groups recognize that any group, regardless of size, is more than the sum of its parts. Groups have a powerful life of their own and can stir up primitive psychic energies with surprising ease. The psychotherapist Wilfred Bion devoted a large part of his professional life to studying groups and what he noticed was that groups seemed to operate at two levels. On the surface most groups had a job to do, and much group activity was naturally organized around this purpose or 'group task'. A school orchestra comes together to play and perform music, a class is created to organize its pupils so that they can learn, a football team comes together in order to play sport and win matches, and so on.

However, Bion also observed that a lot of what goes on in groups was an expression of much more basic human drives and instincts. Despite surface differences, groups were preoccupied with very similar concerns: themes of dominance and control, rivalry and allegiance, belonging and exclusion.

Children need to be alert to the powerful forces groups can stir up in them and those around them. What is going on beneath the surface of the group can cause people to act in an extreme and irrational manner. Groups can generate enormous anxiety amongst their members, and can cause people to act in uncharacteristic ways – hence your child might get on very well with another child when they are alone, but as part of a bigger group, her behaviour might be completely different.

Julia and Samantha were best friends most of the time, but whenever they played together with other children, it was very obvious that Samantha missed no opportunity to put her friend down. She would constantly make 'jokes' about Julia's ginger hair and glasses, and even started parodying certain mannerisms. Quite understandably, Julia became really upset by this.

When Samantha was confronted about her behaviour at first she denied that anything was going on at all. She insisted that it was 'just messing about'. However, later that night her mother found her crying in her room. When she asked her what the matter was, Samantha confessed that she knew that she was hurting her friend's feelings but added: 'I just can't seem to stop myself, Mummy. The other girls think I'm funny but the thing is they're not even my friends – well not like Julia is anyway. I don't know what's wrong with me...'

The answer is simply that Samantha had fallen under the spell of group process. Within the context of this wider circle of acquaintance in which her attachments were less developed, Samantha experienced an intense, irrational anxiety. She tried to compensate for this by desperately attempting to raise her status within the group, unfortunately using Julia as her 'fall guy'. At the time Samantha was not conscious of what she was doing, or why. However, the group affected her so powerfully that even her protective instincts towards her best friend were temporarily overruled.

Bion suggests that all groups churn up primitive, unconscious fantasies. Even placid, mild-mannered children can get caught up in a pack mentality at times.

I am not saying that all experiences driven by group processes are bad. Far from it: some of your child's best moments are likely to be provided by groups – they can foster moments of tender intimacy, invincible solidarity, and bring out some of our best qualities. However, children should be helped to understand that groups can trigger unusual behaviour in others and that they can arouse passions in them that need to be managed responsibly. Forewarned is, to some degree at least, fore-armed.

Scapegoating

In Old Testament Israel the priest would lay hands on a goat and symbolically invest the animal with the sins of the community. The unfortunate goat was then chased out beyond the city wall, in theory carrying the guilt of the city away with it. These days the phrase 'scapegoating' refers to a particularly unpleasant, but commonplace group process that causes many children a great deal of misery.

Groups have a horrible habit of electing one or more members to serve as a convenient bin for the disposal of the group's fears and anxieties. In a case of 'rather him than me' it seems that groups often deal with collective fears about being picked on or thrown out by ostracizing one or more of their own members. For the spectators the bad thing is happening to someone else, and for a while at least this makes everyone else feel a little less on edge.

New group leaders often establish their dominance by casting someone into the role of scapegoat. This also allows them to purchase the favour of the group by temporarily soothing everyone's hidden anxieties. However, for the child to whom this is happening the experience of scapegoating can be horrible, particularly since it is often unclear as to why an individual is being singled out.

Your child needs to be able to recognize scapegoating when it happens and take a firm stand when he encounters it. If he is already using the assertiveness skills outlined in this chapter it is far less likely that he will be picked on.

However, be aware that insecure children vying for high status within the group may feel threatened by an assertive child and be on the look out for opportunities to de-claw a potential rival.

Scapegoating is bullying and needs to be dealt with swiftly and robustly. A child who understands the principle of scapegoating is more likely to spot it in the early stages and take action before it gets out of hand – whether he is the scapegoat or whether he observes the signs that someone else is being positioned in that role. Common signs that scapegoating is taking place include:

- The potential victim becomes the subject of gossip.

- The level of 'good-natured' teasing around the potential scapegoat increases.

- Members of the group may express pseudo-concern about the potential victim and come together either formally or informally to discuss what to do about the 'problem' group member.

- New allegiances are formed within the group designed to exclude the soon-to-be-scapegoated child. High status group members may court the scapegoat's existing allies and friends to lure them away.

- The scapegoat discovers that he is not being given information that he needs to participate fully in the group: no one tells him the time of the party; that he needed to bring his swimming things; that fancy dress was no longer required.

This is all ugly and hurtful stuff, but if a child can spot these tell-tale signs and acts decisively it is possible to abort scapegoating in its early stages. If the process can be exposed for what it is group members may come to their senses and be able to regain conscious control. Assertive communication of feelings by the target victim is key. It is hard to stick the knife in while you are genuinely in touch with someone's suffering.

Scapegoating operates most powerfully in closed groups that have strong boundaries separating them off from the outside world. In William Golding's classic novel *Lord of the Flies* things get really out of hand amongst a group of isolated, shipwrecked school children because they lose contact with any frame of reference beyond the tribal society they have created. If she does see scapegoating occurring, your child should not hold back from telling a teacher or other adult. Apart from anything else, their involvement will break the illusion that the group is sealed off from the outside world and help de-fuse the scape-goating dynamic.

Group roles

The scapegoat is one role into which groups can cast their members but there are many others. Rather like a play in which the parts can be filled by different actors, so the drama of group life tends to throw up the same stereotypes time after time. Common roles include the Rebel, the Clown, the Rescuer, the Gate-keeper and the Conciliator. Each different role performs a specialized function for the group, in much the same way as the different physical organs serve the needs of the whole body. What your child needs to recognize is that groups can often cast children into roles that they wouldn't necessarily choose for themselves. The currents of group life can be very hard to swim against.

When his parents moved to a new town Micah left his junior school with glowing reports. He was regarded by his teachers as a charming, responsible and well-adjusted boy. His sporting ability had made him something of a hero to other children at Midfield Juniors. However, when he joined his new senior school everything changed. Micah never really settled and within a few months his performance in class took a dive. His parents were particularly concerned by reports from Micah's teachers that he had become disruptive in class. Previously a quiet and studious boy, they were now being told that Micah seemed to be drawing attention to himself at every opportunity. If he wasn't deliberately falling off his chair in class he was playing pranks on the teachers or setting off the fire alarm.

His parents wracked their brains to work out what was wrong, but there seemed to be no obvious explanation for this uncharacteristic change in Micah's behaviour. He didn't appear to be worried or depressed. He had generally coped well with the move and said he liked his new school and the friends that he was making there. Concerned that the new friends might be the source of the problem, his parents investigated further. However, according to Micah's teachers his new social circle consisted of industrious, popular children. In fact they were pleased to note that he was getting along particularly well with Lewis, the captain of the football team, whose maturity and strong leadership qualities they felt made him an ideal role model.

Ironically, it turned out that Lewis was the crux of the problem. Within his new group of friends the role that Micah had previously filled in his old school – that of the charismatic leader – had already been filled by Lewis. The group didn't need a new Hero but it did have a vacancy for a Clown. The well-behaved, studious circle of friends badly needed someone to express the manic, madcap energy that they had managed to subdue in themselves.

Without consciously choosing the role for himself, Micah had unwittingly put himself forward. His need to fit in and secure a place within the group was driving him to behave in a way that took everyone by surprise, even Micah himself. It was only by making Micah conscious of what was going on that he was able to start rejecting his new group role and establish a less self-destructive identity for himself.

Ages and stages

Children should also be aware that, just like people, groups go through different stages of development. Entering a group when it is founded is a very different experience from entering a group that has already been established. Tuckman, an academic and researcher, has divided the life of the small group into five (nearly rhyming) stages: forming, storming, norming, performing and adjourning.

As the name suggests, during the 'forming' stage the group comes together. At this point everyone is feeling their way. Group participants tend to be quite open, trying hard to establish connections with other members. Members strive to find similarities and areas of shared experience that can bind the group together. Hostility is rarely expressed at this stage and group members concentrate on gathering information about each other. This is quite a stressful phase and children (and adults) are often not very discriminating about the bonds and alliances they form. There is an opportunistic quality to friendships formed in the early stages of group life that means many of these relationships will either wither or end up being pruned back later on.

The next stage, 'storming', is more turbulent. This is the point at which group members start to feel more at ease with one another and often start jockeying for position, status and power. The storming phase is often accompanied by petty feuds, arguments and bickering.

'Norming' is the phase during which the group establishes the rules, principles and routines by which it will operate. Amongst children these rules are often unspoken and invisible – but children who fall foul of them soon know about it. Most groups are pretty conservative and have little tolerance for members who don't play by the established rules or who challenge the status quo.

I remember watching a group of girls happily playing skipping in a school playground in Lambeth some years ago when another girl tried to join in. She had a skipping rope and her opening gambit was to perform a dazzling series of jumps in front of the other girls. It was an impressive display but, rather than inviting her to join them, the leader of the group fixed a steely eye on the newcomer and announced tartly: 'That isn't how *we* do it here...'

According to Tuckman, once storming and norming have taken place the group is in a position to get on with its appointed task ('performing') until the day inevitably comes when the group must disband. This is the 'adjourning' stage. Just as the formation stage can be stressful, so the disbanding of an established group can evoke deep emotions. If your child is leaving a group that has played a significant part in his life, prepare him for moving on and be sensitive to the strong feelings of loss that children can experience during such endings. Holding a ritual like a leaving party or even a special family meal to mark the event can give your child a sense of closure and provide an opportunity to come to terms with the changes taking place.

Practice makes perfect

This chapter has provided only the briefest introduction to steps you can take to help your child manage his relationships better. However, if your child grasps even some of the principles outlined in these few pages they can make an enormous difference to the quality of the relationships that he forms in life. Where better to learn these skills than within his relationship with you, his parent? Other relationships are much less tolerant, much less forgiving than the one that exists between parent and child. You are ideally placed to provide the sensitive coaching, feedback and support that your child will need as she gets to grips with the difficult business of getting along with others – and staying in control while she does so.

Quick summary action points

- Help your child understand that anger is a normal and healthy emotion, but one that needs to be controlled.

- Make your child familiar with her personal anger 'warning signs' and act quickly when she spots them using the Traffic Light Rule.

- Keep an eye on the motives your child ascribes to others – and any emotionally loaded language he uses to describe situations.

- Train your child to become an assertive communicator:
  —Show him how to use 'I' statements and use appropriate body language to create the right impression.
  —Help your child draw up a personal 'Bill of Rights'.
  —Teach specific assertiveness techniques like 'the broken record' and 'fogging'.
  —Practise the skills of assertive negotiation.

- Give your child insight into the way groups operate:
  —Help her understand processes like scapegoating and know how to deal with them.
  —Make sure she is aware of the way groups can create roles for their members.
  —Support her in dealing with the ages and stages of group life.

7
Unstoppable

Boosting your child's problem-solving skills

In various studies of resilient children, good emotional control and strong problem-solving skills consistently emerge as two characteristics of children who are better at coping with life. In reality these two factors are related: children who don't over-react in a crisis are more likely to retain the presence of mind needed to find a way forward, while children who are confident in their ability to solve problems are less likely to be fazed when difficulties do crop up. Knowing you can cope in a crisis is half the battle to maintaining self-control when things are not going according to plan.

In this chapter we will consider specific problem-solving skills that children can be taught. We will also explore the values and attitudes that will enable your children to encounter frustration and disappointment, without letting their emotions overwhelm them.

Focusing on solutions

Some of the techniques children often find the most helpful in solving their problems come from a field of counselling called Brief Solution-focused Therapy. The hallmark of this approach is not to get bogged down in 'problem-saturated talk' but to concentrate instead on reviewing the occasions when things *do* work out and using your child's existing resources to forge ahead towards solutions.

One tool often used in solution-focused sessions is the so-called 'miracle question'. How this works is that the person with the problem is asked to imagine precisely how life would be different if the problem was already solved.

You can introduce this by asking your child to imagine that they have a magic wand or some other supernatural means of making the problem disappear. Or you can ask them to picture in detail how things would change if they woke up the next morning and the problem had disappeared overnight. What would they be doing differently? How would people around them be reacting? What would be the knock-on effects in other areas of life?

Help your child imagine how she would be behaving if she *didn't* feel so jealous of her sister. When he pictures himself as the self-confident person he ideally wants to be, does your son imagine himself still hanging out with the same gang of unruly mates? If the family was currently getting along as well as it did during that blissful summer holiday in Mallorca, what behaviours would an observer notice more of, and what would he see less of?

The miracle question is actually a neat device for reframing a problem. By standing it on its head, it defines the original problem in terms of its consequences rather than causes. In doing so it translates these consequences into a cluster of mini-problems, each of which can then be tackled in its own right. Although the author and personal development guru Anthony D'Angelo recommends that when dealing with problems you should 'dig at the roots instead of just hacking at the leaves', in practice addressing the results of their difficulties sometimes allows children to find an accessible way in, whereas trying to tackle the source can feel daunting for them. Sometimes a bit of judicious pruning does the job.

The wolf in boy's clothing

Elliot was driving everyone crazy. He was fighting at school, being constantly rude to teachers and his mother and father no longer felt able to manage his behaviour at home. 'He just seems to think he can do what he wants, when he wants ... and if he doesn't get his own way there's all hell to pay. It's so wearing...' confessed his mother while Elliot glared suspiciously from the corner of the consulting room.

Elliot was a much-wanted only child. Sarah, his mother, had suffered several miscarriages before he was born and Elliot had also contracted meningitis as a baby. For a while his parents had thought he might not pull through. Because of these experiences they had found it very hard to be strict with him and had tended to wrap him in cotton wool. Saying 'no' to Elliot was certainly not something that Sarah and Bill were used to.

However, rather than persuading his parents that they needed to take a firmer line with him (which arguably they did) the key was to involve Elliot in solving his own problem. The first step was to help him to see that he had a problem to solve. Once alone, we shifted the focus away from the impact his conduct was having on others and began to think together about the ways in which his behaviour was affecting his life. What was it like when everyone was shouting at him? Did things feel happy at home? Did the teachers treat him differently from everyone else? How did he feel about that? What did he think would happen if it carried on?

Elliot acknowledged that being the Wolf Boy (which was what he called his badly behaved self) did have significant drawbacks as well as advantages. In fact he knew deep inside that he didn't want to be like that. The problem, as he saw it, was that a lot of the time he just felt really angry when people tried to tell him what to do and he wasn't sure he could stop. This was where the miracle question came in. I asked Elliot how he thought his life would change if it was possible to wave a magic wand and he just didn't feel that anger inside him any more?

As Elliot was struggling with this, I asked him to draw a cartoon that showed his life *after* his inner wolf had been removed. Post-lupinectomy, he drew a picture of himself playing happily with his friends on a warm sunny day, another of him sitting attentively in class with his hand up and a frame of his family all holding hands on an outing to Legoland. The images were bright, colourful and cheerful. Elliot shook his head dolefully as he put his pen down: 'I am not that good boy [pointing to himself in the picture]. I don't feel like him any more,' he said glumly.

'Rather than trying to *feel* like him,' I replied, 'do you think you might be able to *do* any of the things you've drawn yourself doing in these pictures? If you had to pretend you were this Elliot, so no one could tell you were still the Wolf Boy inside, what would you need to do? Can you think of any small changes that might make you look a bit more like him on the outside?'

Together we came up with a list of behaviours Elliot would have to adopt in order to convince everyone. He would no longer call out in class. He would walk away when other children tried to pick fights with him. He would go to bed on time without the usual drama. He would say 'please' and 'thank you' rather than demanding and grabbing what he wanted.

Elliot thought this was a hilarious idea – that simply by changing aspects of his behaviour he could 'become' someone else. He was also tickled by how stunned and confused everyone would be if he managed it. I explained that it might not be as easy as he thought, that he might have to do it a bit at a time, but Elliot was up for the challenge.

Two weeks later the family came to see me again. Elliot had done himself proud. 'He's been a different boy ...' his mother announced. 'School has been asking when the old Elliot is coming back.' Later I asked Elliot whether he thought his experiment was working. 'Yes,' he crowed, 'I fooled them all!' Then his tone became accusing: 'But you played a trick on me ... because when I stopped being Wolf Boy on the outside I didn't feel so much like him on the inside any more.' 'Really?' I said innocently, 'And which do you like better?' Elliot rolled his eyes and said nothing. But two months later the Wolf Boy was still nowhere to be seen.

Sometimes, as Elliot's story illustrates, helping a child to shift attention away from the cause of the problem and refocus on what the resolution would look like can point the way to a solution. Many children learn best by doing, so being able to break a problem down into manageable, practical steps often appeals. Looking at the end state after the problem has gone away can help clarify precisely what steps need to be taken.

Ask your child what they would do, how things would be, if they could wave a magic wand. Offer them the chance to draw if that helps. Then help break it down into small practical actions.

Using creative visualization to support problem solving

Children know a lot more than they think they do and are potentially far better at solving all sorts of problems than many adults give them credit for. Unfortunately, our society often sends them the message that they are 'just kids' and teaches them that they stand little chance of arriving at workable solutions without adult help. Consequently, they often doubt their own capabilities.

Paradoxically, children can sometimes be empowered by allowing them to disown their abilities as problem solvers. Helping them create scenarios in which answers and solutions are provided by figures 'outside' themselves can actually enable them to tap into their considerable problem-solving resources.

One way children can learn to do this is through guided visualization. In their imaginations children can be encouraged to consult sources of wisdom for answers and strategies needed to tackle the unresolved situations and difficulties they may be facing.

With children under 7 you can try using the story of the Wise King. Ask the child to imagine herself making a journey through a magical forest with the problem in her backpack. The problem is usually uncomfortable to carry and (maybe a bit sadistically) I suggest that the journey is long and hard. At various points along the way the child is introduced to different characters dwelling in the forest. As she meets various animals, the boy playing by the stream, the old woman baking bread, and so on she asks each of them for help with her problem but always gets the same reply: 'I cannot help you. But I know who can. You need to find the Wise King (or Queen). He is very old and very wise and is sure to be able to help you...'

If you are feeling inventive, each character can provide an example of a problem the Wise King has solved – how he taught the blackbird to fly; the old woman how to put yeast in the bread to make it rise; the boy how to stop people stealing his sweets – and so on. As with all these visualization exercises the elements of repetition and vivid sensual detail help lull your child into a relaxed receptive state. Most children relish the story-telling element of this technique and you can even get them to contribute their own suggestions at this point, a process that can help prime a problem-solving mindset.

Eventually, the child comes to a clearing in the forest and spies a magnificent castle. The drawbridge is lowered and the child is greeted by a steward who says the king is expecting her. The child is taken into an audience with the king who looks appropriately wise and all-knowing ('His eyes are the very deepest, purest blue like a pool so deep you could never reach the bottom even if you could hold your breath for a whole day...'). The child unwraps the problem and presents it to the Wise King who inspects it carefully and gives it due regal consideration.

You then ask your child to imagine that the king is beck-oning her forward and whispering something in her ear so quietly that only she can hear. You could also ask the child to picture the king giving her a gift to help with the problem. The audience with the king ends, the visualization wrapped up and the child gently reoriented to the real world.

After the exercise is over, feel free to ask your child what the Wise King whispered in her ear or what symbolic gift she was given. Occasionally a child will tell you that he didn't really say anything. In this case you nod sagely and say that because the king is so old he does sometimes whisper so quietly that it can indeed be very hard to hear him at first, but that what he said might come back to her later. However, you will often be amazed at the maturity and creativity of some of the king's advice.

One young girl, Jemima, whose brother had suddenly started being mean to her told me gravely that the Wise King had given her a key. When she had used this key to unlock her brother's heart and looked inside she had discovered he was feeling 'very afraid'. Instead of fighting with him any more, she needed to be more understanding. She would tell Spike 'not to be scared', even though she didn't know exactly what was frightening him.

Her mother later told me that the brother was scheduled for a potentially painful medical investigation. It was certainly plausible that Spike's changed behaviour towards his sister had been brought on by underlying anxiety about this. As we saw in Chapter 5, aggression can often be brought on by anxiety and this is exactly what Jemima's intuition was telling her.

Another variation of this technique is widely practised in Neuro-linguistic Programming (NLP). Ask your child to picture someone he really admires or looks up to: a sporting legend, a film star, maybe even a relative. Get your child to imagine the hero figure in an appropriate setting and encourage him to put himself in his hero's shoes so that he has a clear sense of what the person feels like, and what the world looks like through his eyes.

Now ask your child, still in the guise of the hero figure, to step into the problem situation. What does he think about it? How would he handle it? What sort of strategies would he adopt? Seeing the problem from the perspective of someone they already regard as resourceful and competent can help children to analyse the situation in different ways and generate innovative and helpful solutions for themselves.

> Using an imaginary 'somebody else' to solve your child's problem is a useful way of helping them find their own answers.

Map it out

The poet Edward Hodnett claims that: 'A question asked in the right way often points to its own answer.' The same is true of many problems and difficulties routinely faced by children. If children can learn to formulate their difficulties in the right way they are usually more than halfway down the path towards a solution. However, children often present difficulties with key aspects of problem solving: both seeing the bigger picture and breaking the issue down into its component parts, detecting similarities between the structure of old problems and new ones, and appreciating which of the skills and resources that they already have might be relevant.

One tool that can help them overcome these limitations is mind mapping, a technique pioneered by the author and educational consultant Tony Buzan in the 1970s. Mind mapping is now widely used in classroom settings as an aid to helping children learn and remember academic material. However, it is also invaluable in supporting and nurturing children's problem-solving abilities.

The principles behind mind mapping are simple. The map creates a visual image of a subject area that exploits the way the brain encodes information as a network of cascading associations. The average human brain consists of approximately a hundred billion neurons and each individual neuron has connections with hundreds or possibly even thousands of others. Depending on the strength of these individual connections, when one neuron fires it automatically triggers other linked neurons to fire in turn, causing a wave of 'spreading activation' across the network.

Mind mapping mirrors this process on paper. The target subject is represented as a single idea in the middle of a piece of a blank sheet. From this central hub the mind mapper draws out branches representing any new ideas inspired by the original concept. Each of these new ideas can give rise to further associations that are incorporated into the diagram as a network of sub-branches. By freely associating in this way, the mind mapper is quickly able to build up an overview of what she already knows, and of what information she may still need to gather. By using arrows to draw connections between areas and concepts on the map, the individual is also able to see how different aspects of the subject relate to one another.

The process can often spark new insights. Traditional, logical analysis tends to narrow things down, but in mind mapping fresh associations from each node can trigger material that encourages the mind to play freely with ideas. As the connections proliferate, the mind mapper can link up different areas of the map in unexpected new ways. In short, the mind map is a great tool for helping children think creatively about a wide range of situations.

Before moving on to demonstrate how mind mapping can help children solve problems, here are just a few of Buzan's general pointers to help your child get the most out of the mind-mapping process.

- Use images as well as words. Images stimulate the brain in ways that words don't and many children are visual thinkers. By combining words and images Buzan argues that both left and right brain hemispheres are engaged, thereby bringing more brain power to bear on the issue.

- Use colour. Again the brighter and more visually interesting your map becomes, the more likely it is to engage the mapper's attention and creative powers.

- Try and use only single words on each branch. Once words are paired together you restrict the range of associations that individual words/concepts might trigger.

- Try not to censor associations. Productive avenues of thought may come from branches that do not seem immediately relevant. Encourage your child to associate freely.

> Techniques like mind mapping can help an older child to think through the reasons for his problem – and therefore bring possible solutions to the surface.

Late again

In the De Lacey household the day was not getting off to a good start. Kyan (aged 9) was constantly late for school.

For some reason it was proving virtually impossible to get him and his brother Conrad out of the door in enough time to make morning assembly. Kyan was getting into trouble with his teachers, his mother was tearing her hair out and everyone – even Kyan – realized that something needed to change.

Rather than trying to sort the problem out for him Kyan's parents encouraged him to mind map the problem for himself first before they sat down and talked about it together that evening. They knew from experience that this was a good way to get Kyan to take ownership of the problem, think about its various elements and start to work his way towards possible solutions. The map Kyan came up with is recreated overleaf.

When they looked together at Kyan's map, a number of things became clear. By using this technique to structure his problem, Kyan had been able to explore it in some detail and make some important connections between different elements.

One thing Kyan learned was that his lateness appeared to be the result of a number of different factors. These included his forgetfulness, his last-minute approach and the trouble he experienced getting going in the mornings because he was so tired. However, what the mapping process also highlighted was how certain elements had a knock-on effect on each other, keeping the problem going.

For example, the fact that his exasperated mother was getting so irate every morning was putting Kyan under so much stress that it was actually becoming harder for him to concentrate and remember all the things he needed to do. Also, if he did get up late, the fact that other members of his family needed to use the bathroom created an

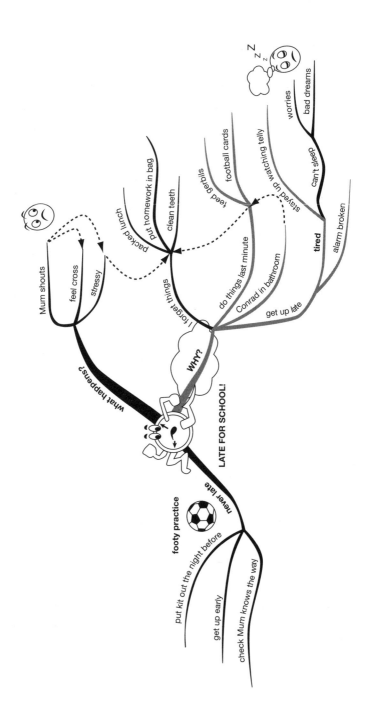

LATE FOR SCHOOL!

what happens?

Mum shouts
feel cross
stressy

put homework in bag
packed lunch
clean teeth
feed gerbils
football cards

stayed up watching telly

WHY?

I forget things
do things last minute
Conrad in bathroom
get up late

tired
can't sleep
worries
bad dreams
alarm broken

never late

footy practice

put kit out the night before
get up early
check Mum knows the way

additional delay so the map revealed that lying in was not an option.

Another helpful aspect of doing the map was that it got Kyan thinking about contrasting situations in which he was *never* late. In doing so he was able to tease out some of the strategies responsible. Getting his football kit ready the night before and borrowing his brother's mobile so he could set an alarm rather than relying on the defunct clock by his bedside were just two steps that meant Kyan was always among the first at his weekly football practice. Kyan realized that he needed to transfer some of these strategies to weekday mornings.

Just thinking about all the different things he needed to do to get ready on schooldays made Kyan appreciate that he needed a plan. He couldn't afford to fumble his way through his morning routine in such a piecemeal, chaotic fashion. At his suggestion his parents agreed to write him a checklist on a whiteboard by the door so that he could do his various tasks in a sensible order and tick them off when they were completed.

However, the most valuable aspect of the mapping process was that it revealed an important dimension of the problem that no one had fully appreciated. It was certainly true that Kyan was tired in the mornings, but it was mind mapping that helped him understand why. Yes, he was staying up far too late watching TV and his parents realized that letting the boys have a television in their room had not been the smartest idea. But the reason for Kyan's late night viewing was that he had been trying to keep himself awake. This was on account of the increasingly anxious thoughts and nightmares he had been having.

This was the crux of the issue. Kyan's sluggish behaviour

in the morning was ultimately a result of his anxious state of mind. Kyan and his parents now realized that they had a very different problem on their hands. Being late for school was just a symptom and it was the mind-mapping process that helped Kyan to identify this. A new set of priorities was clarified and Kyan's parents were then able to support their son in tackling the source of the problem.

Thinking about thinking

Have you ever noticed the different ways children approach tasks? In the *Launchpad* activity centre of the Science Museum in London you will find, amongst other things, a selection of three-dimensional puzzles. Last time we were there I watched several children trying to put them together.

There was a remarkable urgency about some of them. These children just shoved the pieces together in random combinations again and again, obviously hoping that the puzzle would somehow fall into place under their fingers. Needless to say, this wasn't a very successful strategy. Most children who used this approach got nowhere and gave up after just a few minutes. These children knew their internal clock was ticking. Their desperate manipulations became ever more frantic as their rising frustration became intolerable. Some of these children ended up dropping the puzzle as if it was red hot, or angrily scattered the pieces before rushing on to the next attraction.

Other children set about the task in much the same way, manipulating the pieces and trying out different combinations. However, this group were much slower and more deliberate about the process. Every now and again these children would pause and examine what they had done. Sometimes they would retrace their steps and undo bits of the puzzle they had already assembled. Occasionally they would just pick up a piece and study it carefully for a few seconds. When they found a combination that seemed to work, this became part of a construction sequence that they would deliberately repeat. It was obvious that these children were very aware of what they were doing and were learning as they went along. Sometimes they could be heard muttering under their breath: 'This bit can't go here because then that bit won't fit...' Most of these children eventually reached a point of sudden clarity, a 'eureka' moment, after which they quickly and assuredly assembled the puzzle in a few precise movements.

There are some fascinating contrasts between the approaches of these two groups. Both point to the chicken-and-egg nature of the relationship between the ability to keep emotions in check and the capacity to use suitable mental strategies for getting the job done. The fact that children in the first group couldn't handle their frustration made it very hard for them to think straight. For children in the second group it was their confidence in tried and trusted techniques for working things out and their self-aware learning style that enabled them to stay calm. The same principles apply in many everyday situations.

Being conscious of *how* one is achieving results, and being able to review and monitor one's progress, has turned out to be a cornerstone of effective learning. In more progressive educational circles, a group of teachers and researchers have been highlighting the importance of *metacognition* or the ability to think about thinking. These skills come naturally to bright students (or maybe this group has become bright simply because they have always used them?) but the good news for the rest of us is that they can be cultivated.

Gifted kids or gifted mothers?

In a fascinating study in the early 1990s, the Canadian psychologist Ellen Moss and her colleagues compared the way that mothers of exceptionally gifted pre-schoolers talked to them during problem-solving tasks with exchanges between a control group of mothers and children with only average scores on a standard IQ test. Having analysed the strategies the mothers were using, Moss discovered that the mothers of the gifted children were far more likely to be prompting metacognitive strategies than the mothers of the non-gifted children.

These strategies included predicting consequences and thinking about the effect of future actions ('Will this piece fit in that space?'), checking results ('Is that right?'), and reality testing or making meaningful comparisons with what was already known (Should you use such *small* blocks for the foundation?'). Moss also noted that the mothers in the non-gifted group spent more time actively directing their children back to the task, while the gifted children's mothers used activity monitoring: their comments helped their children judge for themselves what kind of progress they were making towards their goal.

Moss speculates whether the giftedness of these children had as much to do with the way their parents were relating to them as with any superior level of inborn intelligence. We cannot be sure. But we do know that amongst populations of school-age children and students, the direct teaching of thinking skills has been shown time and again to produce substantial improvement in academic performance.

Stretch your child's brain power

Obviously the level at which these skills can be taught will depend to some extent on the age of your child. During the pre-school period one of the ways parents can support the development of their child's thinking is by pointing out the features of objects that a child may not spontaneously attend to. Also, while children age 3 and 4 are usually quite capable of following a sequence of simple steps towards a goal, they can find it much harder to hold the bigger picture in mind and keep that end goal in sight. Reminding them of what they are trying to achieve, and refreshing their memory about rules or principles that govern the task can be really useful. Having said this, several researchers believe that between the age of 3 and 5 most children become able to start reflecting on their experience and are therefore ready to start developing key skills like predicting, checking results, self-monitoring and reality testing.

To develop your own child's thinking skills the following pointers may be helpful:

- Do tasks that enable you to think together with your child. Make sure you are thinking out loud: 'What do we need to do next?', 'Is what we're doing now like any other problem we have solved in the past?',

'Let's pause and consider how we're doing for a moment...', 'What are we trying to do here?', 'Can we do anything to help us make better progress?'

- Always start by helping your child recap what he already knows about a subject or problem so that he can make relevant links and connections and give the task a context. Mind maps are great for this.

- Help your child formulate a plan that will enable her to reach the end goal in a series of productive steps. How is she going to tackle the task in hand? What obstacles might she encounter? How will she deal with them?

- Foster the four key metacognitive skills: anticipate; check; monitor; and evaluate.

- Try and help your child see why mastering a particular problem or skill is relevant to his life, and how what he is learning ties in with what he already knows.

- Always encourage your child to evaluate his *own* performance. What was hard about the task? What helped? What has he learned about approaching similar tasks in future?

- As a general rule, try and ask questions to support or provoke your child's thinking rather than issuing directions or providing easy answers. David Hemery, Olympic gold medallist and coach, observes: 'If our questions generate more of their awareness and self-responsibility, the likely result is an increase in our young people's self-belief.'

- Encourage your child to talk to herself as she tackles a task so that she becomes more aware of her own thought processes.

- Be careful not to prompt excessively. Children learn best when they can figure something out for themselves and if you are too quick with a helpful question or reminder they will become reliant on you to do the thinking for them.

- Persuade your child not to rush. Self-awareness, monitoring and in-depth reflection cannot happen if your child is always in a tearing hurry to get to the end. He is also much more likely to make careless mistakes. Model good habits and demonstrate that sometimes it is important to take your time if you really want to understand something properly.

- Finally, always help your child to identify and explicitly label any principles, strategies or rules that are aiding her performance during the task. This enables your child to build up a repertoire of problem-solving skills. Foster the mindset of the French mathematician and philosopher René Descartes who remarked: 'Each problem that I solved became a rule which served afterwards to solve other problems.' Often children deduce and apply principles without being conscious that they are doing so. This makes them less likely to be able to use them in other situations.

Programmed for success

So far in this chapter we have mainly focused on improving thinking skills for effective problem solving. However, people who are good at solving problems and coping well with setbacks do so not just because they possess certain skills, but because they share certain values. Being able to navigate difficulties and dilemmas without losing your cool is ultimately as much a question of attitude as it is of competence. To help children to become truly skilled problem solvers we not only need to equip them with tools and strategies, but also with values to enhance their problem-solving skills.

Researchers studying self-regulation have discovered that people stand a much greater chance of staying in control when they have worked out in advance how they will handle testing situations. Having established protocols already in their heads has been shown to help alcoholics deal better with the temptation to drink and agoraphobics to ward off panic attacks. The values below perform a similar job: they support reliable approach strategies that can keep your child grounded while she explores unfamiliar or emotionally hazardous terrain.

What can I learn here?

One of the most distinctive qualities of world-class problem solvers is the ability to embrace mistakes and setbacks as a valuable aspect of the learning process. The irrepressible Thomas Edison, whose many inventions brought electric light and power into modern homes, was coming from precisely this position when he stated dogmatically: 'I haven't failed. I've found 10,000 ways that don't work.' We need to help our children understand that the problems that initially defeat them are the very ones that have the most to offer them in terms of their personal growth. As Frank Wilczek, the Nobel prize-winning physicist, put it: 'If you don't make mistakes, you're not working on hard enough problems. And that's a big mistake.'

Psychologist Carol Dweck claims that our defensive attitude towards failure is often linked to what she calls the 'fixed' mindset. People with such a mindset tend to see ability as a fixed commodity, predetermined at birth. From such a perspective, failure is always intimidating because our errors disclose to us and everyone else the limits of our talent. They dictate whether we are intelligent or stupid, competent or inept, winners or losers. Children with a fixed mindset constantly compare themselves with others in order to locate themselves on a perceived scale of achievement. Consequently they tend to focus purely on getting results rather than allowing themselves to engage fully with the process of discovery. They also tend to play safe rather than risk the humiliation of failure.

By contrast, Dweck observes that children with a 'growth' mindset seemed positively to relish problems that extended and baffled them. Seen through their eyes, these problems were the ones that provided opportunities for development and could really teach them something. Puzzles that were too easy couldn't do that. These children instinctively believed that far from being fixed, their ability was flexible and could be expanded, but only by constantly pushing their existing boundaries and making sense of their mistakes.

Encourage your child to make friends with failure and respect what it can offer them. Help them cultivate the attitude of John Gardner, the great American administrator and academic, who claimed that: 'We are continually faced with a series of great opportunities brilliantly disguised as insoluble problems.' Celebrate the hard-won victories rather than the easy ones, and help your child mine insights from setbacks in an optimistic and non-judgemental fashion.

> Raise your child to believe that a difficult problem is an exciting prospect and that failure is a step on the path to success.

Stick with it!

'Kids, you tried your best and failed miserably. The lesson is, never try.'

Homer Simpson

Homer's advice to Lisa and Bart is amusing because it stands on its head one of the basic principles of achievement in any field of endeavour. Perseverance far outstrips talent when it comes to deciding who will ultimately master a challenge or overcome an obstacle in life. Calvin Coolidge, the 13th US President, was right when he said 'The slogan "Press On" has solved, and always will solve the problems of the human race,' but helping children develop this kind of stamina is no easy matter.

The pace of the modern world conditions our children to expect everything instantly. Microwaves produce steaming hot meals in a matter of seconds, internet shopping brings goods from all over the world to our door all the year round and most children play computer games that deliver a rapid succession of satisfying 'hits' in return for very little sustained effort. One drawback of this is that today's children often have very little experience of the benefits of perseverance. They have never had opportunities to prove to themselves that it can be worthwhile tolerating frustration and pressing through unyielding circumstances. For such kids, Homer's advice seems eminently sensible.

Not only should you stress the importance of keeping going when things get tough, but try and make sure that your son or daughter is involved in mastering at least one skill that delivers results in proportion to the sustained effort invested in it. Playing a musical instrument is one such activity. Learning to paint or draw is another. Maybe your child has a sporting talent that could be developed? It doesn't matter what it is but, if your child is to hold it together and persevere when he encounters problems, he will need evidence that it can be worthwhile resisting the urge to give up.

> Find a hobby or sport that your child wants to do but that requires perseverance and encourage her to stick at it.

Don't go it alone

When we think of inventors, we usually conjure up an image of some eccentric Professor Branestawm figure alone in his workshop. The reality of effective problem solving is very different. Edison did not invent his famous light bulb on his own. In the course of testing out over 3,000 different materials to find a suitable filament he employed a whole team of research assistants. Einstein used to bounce his latest relativity theories off his physicist wife, Mileva Maric, and at the turn of the 19th century Marie Curie made her pioneering discoveries into radioactivity in collaboration with her husband Pierre.

Help your children to appreciate that intelligent problem solving often means involving other people and making the most of their knowledge and experience. Simply having to communicate the issues to someone else will require them to begin organizing their ideas, and having someone on hand to act as a sounding board can also help them evaluate possible solutions.

Encourage your child to share her problems with you but when she does try and resist the temptation to 'take over' and deliver a solution. It will be far more helpful for your child in the long term if you can support and nurture her own problem-solving potential by giving constructive feedback on her efforts to find a way forward.

Never assume

In 1986 when the space shuttle *Challenger* exploded in a ball of flame 73 seconds after lift-off, the American government commissioned a thorough investigation into the causes of the accident. A key figure in the investigation was Professor Richard Feynman, one of the most original and incisive minds of his generation. What Feynman's investigations revealed was shocking: managers at NASA had pushed ahead with the launch despite warnings from the technical team that the O-ring seals on the solid rocket boosters were potentially faulty and that the cold weather might cause significant problems for the shuttle. The managers simply assumed that everything would go smoothly. They saw only what they wanted to see, even though the people who knew best were telling them their analysis of the situation was skewed. The result was the unnecessary death of seven astronauts.

Outstanding problem solvers are often the people who challenge the assumptions everyone else takes for granted. They take account of all the information they have at their disposal, not just the bits that fit with their existing model of the world. They do not rely on hearsay or second-hand knowledge when it contradicts the evidence of their own observations or powers of reasoning.

Feynman wrote how grateful he was to his father for teaching him how to make careful observations of the natural world, unclouded by preconceptions about what he would see. Leonardo da Vinci's outstanding scientific and artistic genius also found a common root in his capacity to look at what was in front of him unblinkered by conventional wisdom.

In allowing themselves to 'think outside the box' these individuals were able to see more clearly into the true nature of things and come up with some impressively innovative solutions. This is an invaluable quality for good problem solvers to possess because as Albert Einstein drily pointed out: 'The significant problems we have cannot be solved at the same level of thinking with which we created them.' On a practical level, if what your child is doing currently isn't working, encourage him to try something else!

> Encourage children to question everything, challenge assumptions, think about problems in different ways and be creative.

Also, train your children to feel at ease with uncertainty. In a televised interview Richard Feynman emphasized how important it is for good scientists to be comfortable with doubt and 'not knowing' and the same applies to budding problem solvers. Teach your children to think through situations for themselves and ensure that they are taking into account all the relevant facts. Foreclosing and rushing to a half-baked solution is seldom a productive way to proceed. Encourage them to question everything and hold all 'certainties' lightly. In doing so you will encourage flexible thinking that will produce creative responses to even the most difficult challenges life throws at them.

 ## Quick summary action points

- Encourage your child to focus on solutions using techniques like the 'miracle question' and reframe complex problems in manageable terms.

- Help your child tap into his own problem-solving powers by allowing him to recruit 'outside' help in the form of an imaginary mentor.

- Teach your child how to explore and structure problems using tools like mind mapping.

- Train your child to become aware of the processes that underlie productive thinking and successful problem solving:

—Think aloud with your child.

—Develop the four key skills: Anticipate ... Check ... Monitor ... and Evaluate.

—Ask questions that allow your child to find her own solutions.

—Help your child take note of the strategies that work.

- Cultivate the mindset and values of world-class problem-solvers: perseverance, collaboration, open-mindedness and curiosity.

And finally . . . happily ever after?

'Feelings are real and legitimate; children behave and misbehave for a reason, even if adults cannot figure it out.'

Author unknown

This book was written with three goals in mind. The first was to try and help parents understand the reasons why children misbehave and I urge you to keep grappling with the underlying causes. Despite what you may have seen on television, when it comes to successful parenting there are no quick fixes.

Secondly, I wanted to make the point that the skirmishes we have with our offspring pale into insignificance compared with the internal battles our children are waging against their own feelings and impulses. Although the landscape of childhood can feel alien to grown-ups at times, we need to understand the minds and hearts of our children if we are to become useful allies in their battle for self-control.

Lastly, I hoped to convince you that we are long overdue for a shift in the parenting agenda. We need to set our sights beyond the management of children's behaviour and embrace the broader opportunities and privileges that parenthood offers. This book tries to map out a wider definition of parental 'discipline' and acknowledge our duty to equip children with the psychological skills they need to behave well and – more importantly – to live well.

How well these aims have been achieved only you can judge. Nevertheless, we should probably all pay heed to the words of Jackie Onassis who stated that: 'If you bungle raising your children, I don't think whatever else you do well matters very much.' It is tough then that parenting well turns out to be such a demanding business. I certainly can't afford to put myself on any pedestal as a parent (as my wife and sons will be quick to tell you!) and am often just as beleaguered as the next struggling dad. However, working as a psychologist has given me some faith in the transformations that can be achieved if children are equipped with the tools they need to begin mastering their emotional lives.

I trust you will feel inspired to try out the techniques described in these pages for yourself and, at the very least, that the journey will bring you and your child closer. The author G. K. Chesterton once remarked that he liked children '... if they're properly cooked'. My hope is that in these pages you will find some recipes that will be of some use to you both along the way.

References and further reading

Bandura, A. (1977) 'Self-efficacy: Toward a unifying theory of behaviour change'. *Psychological Review*, 84, 191–215.

Baumeister, R. F. (1997) 'Esteem threat, self-regulatory breakdown, and emotional distress as factors in self-defeating behaviour'. *Review of General Psychology*, 1, 145–174.

Baumeister, R. F., Bratslavsky, E., Muraven, M. and Tice, D. M. (1998) 'Ego Depletion: Is the Active Self a Limited Resource?'. *Journal of Personality and Social Psychology*, 74, 1252–1265.

Baumeister, R. F. and Vohs, K. D. (2004) *Handbook of Self-regulation – Research, Theory and Applications*. The Guilford Press: London.

Berk, L. E. and Winsler, A. (1995) 'Scaffolding Children's Learning: Vygotsky and Early Childhood Education'. Washington, DC: National Association for the Education of Young Children. ERIC Document No. ED384443.

Bourne, E. J. (2005) *The Anxiety and Phobia Workbook*. New Harbinger Publications: Oakland CA.

Bransford, J. D., Brown, A. L. and Cocking, R. (eds) (2000) *How People Learn*. National Academy Press: Washington DC.

Brown, A. L. (1987) 'Metacognition, executive control, self-regulation, and other more mysterious mechanisms'. In F. E. Weinert and R. H. Kluwe (eds) *Metacognition, Motivation and Understanding*. Lawrence Erlbaum Associates: New Jersey.

Butler, G. (1999) *Overcoming Social Anxiety and Shyness: A Self-help Guide Using Cognitive Behavioral Techniques*. Robinson: London.

Buzan, T. (2003) *Mind Maps for Kids: An Introduction*. Thorsons: London.

Coleman, J. C. and Hendry, L. B. (1999) *The Nature of Adolescence*. Routledge: London.

Dapretto, M. (2006) 'Understanding emotions in others: mirror neuron dysfunction in children with autism spectrum disorders'. *Nature Neuroscience*, 9(1), 28–30.

Davies, W. (2000) *Overcoming Anger and Irritability*. New York University Press: New York.

Day, J. (1994) *Creative Visualization with Children*. Element Books: Shaftesbury.

De Bono, E. (1993) *Teach Your Child How to Think*. Penguin Books: London.

Doyle Gentry, W. (2007) *Anger Management for Dummies*. Wiley: New Jersey.

Dweck, C. S. (1999) *Self-Theories: Their Role in Motivation, Personality, and Development*. Taylor and Francis: Philadelphia.

Dweck, C. (2006) *Mindset: The New Psychology of Success*. Random House: New York.

Edwards, D. (1962) *My Naughty Little Sister's Friends*. Egmont: London.

Eisenberg, N., Lennon, R. and Roth, K. (1983) 'Pro-social development: a longitudinal study'. *Developmental Psychology*, 19(6), 846–855.

Faber, A. and Mazlish, E. (2002) *How to Talk so Kids will Listen and Listen so Kids will Talk*. HarperCollins: New York.

Fennell, M. (1999) *Overcoming Low Self-esteem*. Robinson: London.

Feynman, R. P. (1992) *Surely You're Joking Mr Feynman! Adventures of a curious character*. Vantage: London.

Friedberg, R. D. and McClure, J. M. (2002) *Clinical Practice of Cognitive Therapy with Children and Adolescents – The Nuts and Bolts*. The Guilford Press: London.

Gallo, D. (1989) 'Educating for Empathy, Reason and Imagination'. *The Journal of Creative Behaviour*, 23(2), 98–115.

Goleman, D. (1996) *Emotional Intelligence: Why it can matter more than IQ*. Bloomsbury: London.

Greenberger D. and Padesky C. A. (1995) *Mind Over Mood: Change how you feel by changing the way you think*. The Guilford Press: New York.

Gurvits, T. V., Shenton, M. E., Hokama, H., Ohta, H., Orr, S. P., Lasko, N. B., et al (1996) 'Magnetic resonance imaging study of hippocampal volume in chronic, combat-related post-traumatic stress disorder.' *Biological Psychiatry*, 40: 1091–1099.

Hargie, O. and Dickson, D. (2004) *Skilled Interpersonal Communication: Research, Theory and Practice*. Routledge: London.

Harris, J. (1999) *The Nature Assumption*. Bloomsbury: London.

Hartley, M. (2005) *The Assertiveness Handbook*. Sheldon Press: London.

Hawton, K., Salkovskis, P. M., Kirk, J. and Clark, D. M. (1989) *Cognitive Behaviour Therapy for Psychiatric Problems – A Practical Guide*. Oxford University Press: Oxford.

Hemery, D. (2005) *How to Help Children Find the Champion within Themselves*. BBC Worldwide: London.

Henley, M. (2003) *Teaching Self-Control: A Curriculum for Responsible Behavior*. National Education Service: Bloomington.

Higgins, S., Hall, E., Baumfield, V. and Moseley, D. (2005) 'A meta-analysis of the impact of the implementation of thinking skills approaches on pupils'. In: *Research Evidence* in Education Library, EPPI-Centre, Social Science Research Unit, Institute of Education, University of London.

HMSO (2005) 'Mental Health of Children and Young People in Great Britain, 2004' (Crown copyright).

Iannotti, R. J. (1978) 'Effect of role-taking experiences on role taking, empathy, altruism & aggression'. *Developmental Psychology*, 14 (2), 119–124.

Lair, J. (1995) *I Ain't Much, Baby – But I'm All I've Got*. Fawcett Books.

Lezak, M. D. (1995) *Neuropsychological Assessment*. Oxford University Press: Oxford.

Lucas, B. and Smith A. (2002) *Help Your Child to Succeed: the essential guide for parents*. Network Educational Press Ltd: Stafford.

Malan, D. H. (1997) *Individual Psychotherapy and the Science of Pyschodynamics*. Butterworth Heinemann: Oxford.

Maslow, A. H. (1968) *Toward a Psychology of Being*. Van Nostrand Reinhold: New York.

McMullin R. E. (2000) *The New Handbook of Cognitive Therapy Techniques*. Norton: New York.

Mills, R. S. and Grusec, J. E. (1989) 'Cognitive, affective and behavioural consequences of praising altruism'. *Merrill-Palmer Quarterly*, 35(3), 299–326.

Mischel W. (1974) 'Processes in Delay Gratification'. In L. Berkowitz (ed.) *Advances in Experimental Social Psychology*, 7, 249–292. C. A. Academic Press: San Diego.

Mischel W., Shoda, Y. and Rodriguez, M. I. (1989) 'Delay of gratification in children'. *Science*, 244 (4907), 933–938.

Moore, B. E. and Fine, B. D. (eds) (1995) *Psycho-Analysis, The Major Concepts*. Yale University Press: London.

Moss, E. S., and Strayer, F. F. (1990) 'Interactive problem-solving of mothers and gifted and nongifted preschoolers'. *International Journal of Behavioral Development*, 13(2), 177–197.

Nettle, D. (2007) *Personality: What Makes You the Way You Are*. Oxford University Press: Oxford.

Payne, R. A. (2002) *Relaxation Techniques: A Practical Handbook for the Healthcare Professional*. Churchill Livingstone: Edinburgh.

Rizzolatti, G. and Graighero, L. (2004) 'The mirror-neuron system'. *Annual Review of Neuroscience*, 2204 (27), 169–192.

Sax, L. (2005) *Why Gender Matters: What Parents and Teachers need to Know About the Emerging Science of Sex Differences*. Doubleday: London.

Segal, Z. V., Williams, J. M. G. and Teasdale, J. D. (2002) *Mindfulness-based Cognitive Therapy for Depression: A New Approach to Preventing Relapse*. The Guilford Press: New York.

Selekman, M. D. (1993) *Pathways to Change: Brief Therapy Solutions with Difficult Adolescents*. The Guilford Press: London.

Selekman, M. D. (1997) *Solution-focused Therapy with Children: Harnessing family strengths for systemic change*. The Guilford Press: London.

Seligman, M. (1995) *The Optimistic Child: Proven Program to Safeguard Children from Depression & Build Lifelong Resilience*. HarperCollins: New York.

Shuster, C. (2000) 'Emotions Count: Scaffolding Children's Representations of Themselves and Their Feelings to Develop Emotional Intelligence'. In: *Issues in Early Childhood Education: Curriculum, Teacher Education, & Dissemination of Information*. Proceedings of the Lilian Katz Symposium (Champaign, IL, 5–7 November 2000).

Skinner, B. F. (1988) *About Behaviorism*. Random House: New York.

Smith, C. and Nylund, D. (1997) *Narrative Therapies with Children and Adolescents*. The Guilford Press: London.

Staricoff, M. and Rees, A. (2005) *Start Thinking: Daily Starters to inspire thinking in primary classrooms*. Imaginative Minds: Birmingham.

Stern, D. N. (1985) *The Interpersonal World of the Infant: A view from psychoanalysis and Developmental Psychology*. Basic Books: New York.

Stiles, J. (2000) 'Neural plasticity and Cognitive Development'. *Developmental Neuropsychology*, 18(2), 237–272.

Tangney, J. P., Baumeister, R. F. and Boone, A. (2004) 'High Self-control predicts good adjustment, less pathology, better grades, and interpersonal success'. *Journal of Personality*, 72, 271–324.

Tice, D. M., Bratslavsky, E. and Baumeister, R. (2001) 'Emotional Distress Regulation Takes Precedence Over Impulse Control: If You

Feel Bad, Do It!' *Journal of Personality and Social Psychology*, 80(1), 53–67.

Travers P. L. (1934) *Mary Poppins*. HarperCollins: London.

Tuckman, B. W., and Jensen, M. A. C. (1977) 'Stages of small group development revisited', *Group and Organizational Studies*, 2, 419–427.

Valiente, C., Eisenberg, N., Fabes, R. A., Shepard, S. A., Cumberland, A. and Losoya, S. H. (2004) 'Prediction of children's empathy-related responding from their effortful control and parent's expressivity'. *Developmental Psychology*, 40(6), 911–926.

Vernon, D. T. A. and Blake, R. L. (1993) 'Does problem-based learning work? A meta-analysis of evaluative research'. *Academic Medicine*, 68, 550–563.

Vygotsky, L. S. (1986) *Thought and Language* (A. Kozulin, Trans.). MIT Press: Cambridge, MA.

Weinberger, D. R., Elvevåg, B. and Giedd, J. (2005) *The Adolescent Brain: A Work in Progress*. The National Campaign to Prevent Teen Pregnancy.

Wells, A. (1997) *Cognitive Therapy of Anxiety Disorders: a practice manual and conceptual guide*. Wiley and Sons: Chichester.

Werdmann, A. M. (1976) *Words and Feelings: Children's Vocabulary of Selected Emotions*. Dissertation thesis. ERIC no. 132612.

Winnicott, D. W. (1958) *Collected Papers*. Tavistock Publications: London.

Wood, D. J., Bruner, J. and Ross, G. (1976) 'The role of tutoring in problem solving'. *Journal of Child Psychology and Psychiatry*, 17(2), 89–100.

Wood, D. (1998) *How Children Think and Learn*. Blackwell: Oxford.